THE WORLD OF ANIMALS

VOLUME 2

© Macmillan Publishers Limited 1990
Artwork © BLA Publishing Ltd 1990

All rights reserved. No reproduction, copy or transmission of this publication may be made without written permission.

No paragraph of this publication may be reproduced, copied or transmitted save with written permission or in accordance with the provisions of the Copyright Act 1956 (as amended), or under the terms of any licence permitting limited copying issued by the Copyright Licensing Agency, 33–4 Alfred Place, London WC1E 7DP.

Any person who does any unauthorised act in relation to this publication may be liable to criminal prosecution and civil claims for damages.

First published in 1986 in three volumes: Life in the Wild, Life in the Water, On the Wing

Published by
Macmillan Children's Books
A division of
MACMILLAN PUBLISHERS LTD
Houndmills, Basingstoke, Hampshire RG21 2XS
and London
Companies and representatives throughout the world

Designed and produced by BLA Publishing Limited,

Printed in Hong Kong

British Library Cataloguing in Publication Data

The world of animals
1. Animals
591
ISBN 0–333–51138–7 Vol 2

Photographic credits
t = top b = bottom l = left r = right

cover: Christian Zuber/Bruce Coleman

8 Anthony Bannister/NHPA; 9 Ed Lawrenson; 10 Peter Johnson/NHPA; 11*t* Aquila; 13 J & M Bain/NHPA; 16 John Shaw/NHPA; 17*b* Ivan Polunin/NHPA; 18 Michael Leach/NHPA; 19*b* Aquila; 20, 21 Seaphot; 24*t* Douglas Baglin/NHPA; 24*b* ZEFA; 25 L.H. Newman/NHPA; 27 Philip Wayre/NHPA; 28*b* Manfred Danegger/NHPA; 30 Eero Murtomaki/NHPA; 31*t* John Shaw/NHPA; 31*b*, 32, 33*t* Aquila; 33*b* Ed Lawrenson; 34*t*, 34*b* Aquila; 36 John Shaw/NHPA; 37 Brian Hawkes/NHPA; 38/39, 39*t* Peter Johnson/NHPA; 39*b* Antony Bannister/NHPA; 40, 41*t*, 41*b* Stephen Dalton/NHPA; 42 Grospas Nature/NHPA; 43*t* Peter Johnson/NHPA; 43*b* S. Krasemann/NHPA; 44*t* Aquila; 44*b* Brian Hawkes/NHPA; 45 Fotocentre/NHPA; 46, 47*t* ZEFA; 47*b* Aquila; 48 Jany Sauvanet/NHPA; 49*t* Aquila; 49*b* E. Hanumantha Rao/NHPA; 52 Warren Williams/Seaphot; 55*t* Peter David/Seashot; 53*b* Peter Johnson/NHPA; 54 M.I. Walker/NHPA; 55*t* Peter David/Seaphot; 55*b* Pete Atkinson/Seaphot; 56*t* Peter Vine/Seaphot; 57*t* Alex Kerstitch/Seaphot; 57*b* M.D. Griffiths/Seaphot; 60 Alex Kerstitch/Seaphot; 61*t* Peter David/Seaphot 61*b*; Herwarth Voigtmann/Seaphot; 62*t* David Maitland/Seaphot; 62*b* David George/Seaphot; 63 Alex Kerstitch/Seaphot; 64*t* Richard Chesher/Seaphot; 64*b* Anthony Bannister/NHPA; 65 Mick Laverack/Seaphot; 71*t*, 71*b* Ken Lucas/Seaphot; 72 Christian Petron/Seaphot; 73*t* Ken Lucas/Seaphot; 73*b* Roy Manstan/Seaphot; 74*t* Richard Chesher/Seaphot; 74*b* Alex Kerstitch/Seaphot; 75 Peter Scoones/Seaphot; 76 C.S.Milkins/Aquila; 77*t* Jim Greenfield/Seaphot; 77*b* Christian Petron/Seaphot 80*t* Peter Scoones/Seaphot; 80*b* Geoff Harwood/Seaphot; 81 Peter Scoones/Seaphot; 82*t* Warren Williams/Seaphot; 83 Herwarth Voigtmann/Seaphot; 84/85, 85*t* Peter David/Seaphot; 86 Gilbert van Ryckevorsel/Seaphot; 87*t* John and Gillian Lythgoe/Seaphot; 88*t* G.I. Bernard/NHPA; 88*b* M.Walker/NHPA; 89 Steve Nicholls/Seaphot; 92 Chris Howes/Seaphot; 93*t* Warren Williams/Seaphot; 93*b* G. I. Bernard/NHPA; 96 Philip Shaw/NHPA; 97 ANT/NHPA; 104*b* Manfred Daneggar/NHPA; 105*b* Peter Johnson/NHPA; 107 Philippa Scott/NHPA; 108*t* Peter Castell/Aquila; 108*b* E. Hanumantha Rao/NHPA; 110*t* Stephen Dalton/NHPA; 110*b* M.F. Soper/NHPA; 111 Brian Hawkes/NHPA; 112 Hellio & Van Ingen/NHPA; 113*t* Brian Hawkes/NHPA; 114 Philippa Scott/NHPA; 115*t* Joe B. Blossom/NHPA; 115*b* Brian Hawkes/NHPA; 116 Wayne Lankinen/Aquila; 117*t* Roger Tidman/NHPA; 117*b* Bryan Sage/Aquila; 119*t* M.C. Wilkes/Aquila; 119*b* N. Williams/Aquila; 120 Bryan Sage/Aquila; 121*t* Stephen Krasemann/NHPA; 122*t* Peter Johnson/NHPA; 122*b* J.J. Brookes/NHPA; 123 R.J. Erwin/NHPA; 124/125 Stephen Krasemann/NHPA; 124*b* Stephen Dalton/NHPA; 125 Haroldo Palo Jr/NHPA; 126 A.T. Moffett/Aquila; 127*b* R.J. Erwin/NHPA; 128 Philip Wayre/NHPA; 129*t* A. Sutherland/Aquila; 129*b* G.D.T./NHPA; 130 J. Jeffery/NHPA; 131*t* R.W. Knightbridge/NHPA; 131*b* Brian Hawkes/NHPA 132 L. Campbell/NHPA; 133*t* Patrick Fagot/NHPA; 133*b* L. Campbell/NHPA; 134 Aquila; 135, 136 M.F. Soper/NHPA; 137*t* James Hancock/Aquila

Note to the reader
In this book there are some words in the text which are printed in **bold** type. This shows that the word is listed in the glossary on page 182. The glossary gives a brief explanation of words which may be new to you.

THE WORLD OF ANIMALS

VOLUME 2

M
MACMILLAN

Contents

Life in the wild

Introduction	8
Survival in the wild	10
Seashore life	12
Life in lakes and rivers	14
Life in wet lands	16
Grasslands of the north	18
Grasslands of South America	20
Grasslands of Africa	22
Grasslands of Australia	24
Animals in rain forests	26
Animals in woodlands	28
Animals in pine forests	30
Life in the coldest places	32
Animals that hibernate	34
Mountain animals	36
Desert animals	38
Animals of the night	40
Animals on the move	42
Animals on islands	44
Taming wild animals	46
Wildlife in danger	48

Life in the water

Introduction	52
The simplest animals	54
Jellyfish and sea anemones	56
Life in a shell	58
Octopuses and squids	60
Crabs and their relatives	62
Starfish and sea urchins	64
What is a fish?	66
Breathing and moving	68
Fish without jaws	70
Sharks and rays	72
Bony fish	74
Protection from enemies	76
Ocean layers	78
Life near the coast	80
Coral reefs	82
Deep sea animals	84
The long journeys	86
Life in fresh water	88
Freshwater fish	90
Water animals in danger	92

On the wing

Introduction	96
The first birds	98
Thousands of types	100
A bird's body	102
How birds fly	104
Dance and courtship	106
Nests and eggs	108
The young bird	110
The long journeys	112
The polar regions	114
Seabirds	116
Wetland birds	118
Birds in the open	120
Birds in deserts	122
Birds in rain forests	124
Birds in woodlands	126
The northern forests	128
Mountain birds	130
City life	132
Birds on islands	134
Birds in danger	136
Glossary	138
Index	143

LIFE IN THE WILD
Elizabeth Oakley

Introduction

We share our planet with millions of other animals. We give some of them food and shelter. Some, like horses or camels, are tamed. Others, like sheep and cattle, we keep on farms. We call these types of animals **domestic animals**. Most animals on Earth are wild animals. They have to find their own food and know how to protect themselves.

Places to live

The place where an animal lives is called its **habitat**. Animals can live in holes in trees, under pebbles or high up in a mountain stream. Animals live in every nook and cranny on Earth.

Many things affect the habitat of plants and animals. Is it hot or cold? What type of soil is there? How high is it? Is it close to the sea, or **inland**? All these things add up to make the animal's surroundings, or **environment**.

▼ The African elephant lives in a hot, dry habitat. Its large ears keep it cool.

Introduction

Elephant seals live in surroundings very different from the African elephants. Their bodies are covered with thick blubber to keep out the bitter cold.

Millions of types

Millions of types, or **species**, of animals live on Earth. Scientists do not yet know all of them. Some animals are very tiny and often have only one part or **cell**. An example is the **amoeba** (*am-ee-ba*), which is a tiny speck of live jelly. The largest animal is the blue whale, over 30 m long!

Each type of animal fits into one type of environment. Some animals live in hot deserts. A few, like the polar bear, prefer the cold. On Mount Everest, 8000 m above sea level, lives a small bird that looks like a crow. At a depth of 8000 m below sea level, lives an unusual fish called a tripod fish. Some places attract more types of animals than others. Thousands of types live on coral reefs. The greatest mixture of types of animals live in hot, steamy jungles.

All these animals have become used to a life in one type of place. Their shape, size, colour, food needs and skills have changed over thousands of years to suit life in that habitat. This change is called **adaptation**.

Survival in the wild

▼ A lioness gives chase. There is only a small chance that she will catch and kill one of these giraffes. The long legs and heavy hoofs of the giraffes could knock the lioness down. The lioness is taking the chance because she needs food. Staying alive is not easy, even for her.

Have you ever been really cold or hungry? The answer is likely to be 'no'. Most of us eat every day and sleep in warm beds at night. In the wild, it is not the same. Animals often have to struggle to eat and find shelter. They must always look out for danger. Most animals end up as food for another type of animal.

Staying alive

Animals defend themselves in many ways. Some have a tough armour, like tortoises. Other animals have weapons, like the horns of a goat. A few animals are poisonous, like some tropical frogs. Some pretend to be fierce. The owlet moth has wings with huge 'eyes' on them. These

Survival in the wild

▲ Most animals need to keep a constant look out for enemies. A rabbit has no defence against an attacker, so it must either hide or run. Even so, the rabbit family is one of the most successful groups of wild animals. Rabbits breed very quickly and can live in all sorts of climates.

eyes frighten attackers. Deer can run very fast. This allows them to escape from their enemies.

One way of staying alive is not to be seen at all. Many animals blend in with the leaves, rocks and soil around them. Some insects look like twigs. These insects are **camouflaged**.

Animals that hunt other animals are called **predators**. They have to chase, catch and kill their prey. The predators need speed, strength and strong teeth to do this. Look at a cat's teeth. Imagine those daggers, twenty times bigger, in a cheetah. All is well for a predator until it is not able to catch its **prey**. If a cheetah breaks a leg, or goes blind, what happens then?

A natural order

In this struggle for life in the wild, there is an order. This order begins with the sun. Plants use light from the sun to make their food. Animals do not do this. They have to eat plants, or other animals.

The sun is the first link in a chain. This chain is called a **food chain**. There are many other links to look at. Think of a pond. On the pond are water lilies. A butterfly takes **nectar** from the lilies. The butterfly is snapped up by a dragonfly. Suddenly the long tongue of a frog lashes out. It grabs the dragonfly. In the grass nearby lies a snake. The frog is eaten by the snake. Then, like a feathered torpedo, an eagle rushes to earth. After a good fight, it kills the snake.

Most animals in this chain have eaten another animal. The only plant eater is the butterfly. In the end, they all depend on the plant.

▲ All life depends on some other form of life for food. Plants supply food for plant eaters. Plant eaters then become meals for meat eaters. Without plants, the plant eaters could not survive, nor could the meat eaters.

Seashore life

There are many types of seashore. Even along a short stretch of coast there can be rocky, pebbly, sandy or muddy shores. What type of rock is the shore made of? Is it hard or does it crumble? Waves slowly wear away the rock, whatever the type. The waves may wash the small pieces of rock, or pebbles, along the coast. The pebbles rub together and break into large sand grains. Where fine sand collects, flat beaches are formed.

High and low tides

Twice a day, the sea creeps up the land and goes back again. This rise and fall is called the **tide**. When the sea reaches its highest point, it is high tide. When the sea is at its lowest point, it is low tide. The tides are caused by the pull of the moon and the sun.

Sandy beaches

Many small animals live on sandy beaches. If you look into the water at high tide you may see shrimps, crabs or jellyfish. They all disappear at low tide. Some burrow under the sand where it is safe. Below the surface the sand stays damp, which they like.

This picture shows animals on a rocky shore when the tide is out. Limpets, mussels and barnacles cling to the rocks. A rock pool has become home for a starfish and a shrimp. In the pool, sea anemones fan out their tentacles. Lugworms and cockles bury themselves in the sand. An oyster catcher patrols the beach in search of cockles. It will use its strong beak to break open the cockle shells.

Seashore life

► The shore crab, seen here, blends very well with its surroundings. It is a poor swimmer, and spends most of its time crawling through rock pools. It feeds on small animals.

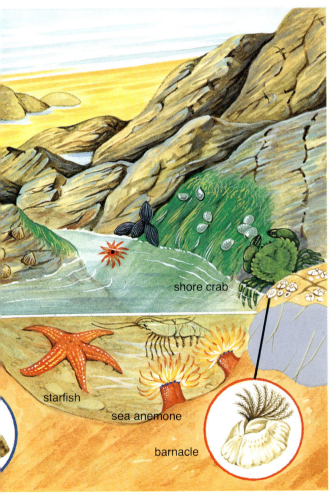

Lugworms sift through the sand for food. They leave coils of sand behind them, which you may see at low tide. Wading birds, such as oyster catchers and snipe, walk along the sand. Their long beaks poke down in search of the small animals. They also go through the rubbish, or **debris**, left on the beach by the waves.

Rocky beaches

Rocky beaches have many more types of animals than sandy beaches. At high tide, animals cannot burrow into the sand to escape the crashing of the waves. So they must have strong shells and be able to cling to the rocks. Some, like mussels and scallops, hang on with tough 'ropes'. Others, like limpets and barnacles, hang on with a broad sucker.

When the tide goes out, small pools of water are left among the rocks. The pools are full of life. In the rock pools are small fish and crabs. Sea anemones cling to the rocks. Underwater they fan out their tentacles to catch their prey. Starfish move slowly around. They are strong enough to break open and eat the shellfish.

Life in lakes and rivers

Water inland is known as fresh water. Fresh water does not contain as much salt as the sea. Most animals who live in water are used to either a life in the sea, or to a life in fresh water. A few can live in both. In fresh water there are many types of habitat.

Streams and rivers

Life in a river changes along its length. A river can be divided into different parts, or **reaches**. Reaches often start in the mountains. The upper reach of a river is steep, with boulders. The cold water rushes along, carrying small stones with it. Few plants and animals can get a grip. Plants, called **algae**, and insect **larvae** cling to the boulders. Only strong fish like salmon can survive.

Water in the middle reach still flows swiftly, but it drops the small stones or gravel. Plants have a chance of getting a grip in the gravel. Most animal life exists where gravel collects. Snails and larvae with flat bodies, like mayfly, live among the plants. Fish, such as trout, live in the middle reach too. They are strong swimmers and have a good shape for pushing through the current.

In the low reach, the water slows and warms up. The land is flat and there are no rocks. The river drops fine mud, or **silt**, which it has carried from the mountains. Burrowing in the silt are clams, worms and turtles. Many plants grow in the low reach. The fish have narrow bodies so they can slip through the plants.

▼ Some of the life found along the length of a northern river. In the upper reach, salmon and a few insect larvae live in the fast flowing water. In the middle reach, trout, snails and mayfly larvae are found. In the low reach, tench, chub, turtles, clams and worms are found.

UPPER REACH

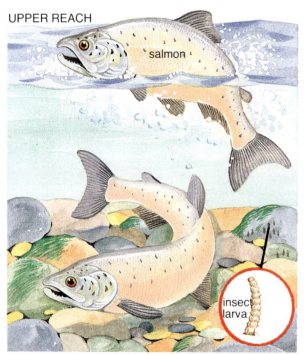

MIDDLE REACH

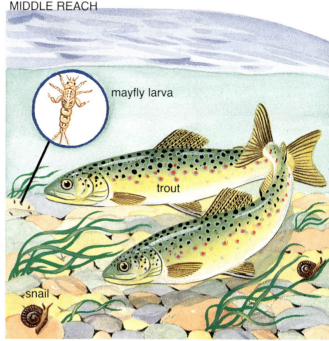

Life in lakes and rivers

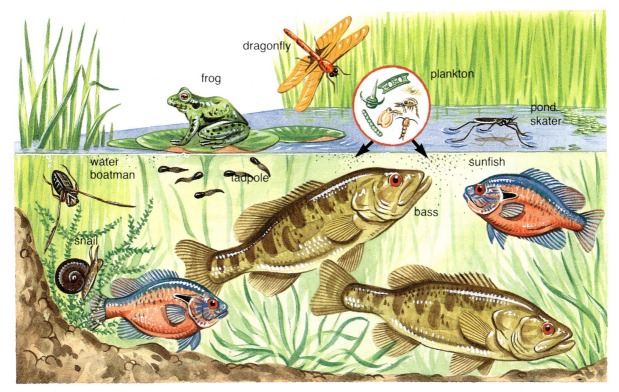

▲ A wide range of plant and animal life is found in a pond. The water is still, which means that the plants and animals do not have to struggle against flowing water. Tiny plants and animals float near the surface. These are food for larger animals, such as bass. The other animals include insects and amphibians.

Lakes and ponds

Lakes are larger and deeper than ponds. In the middle of lakes, there is little plant life. A lake can be split into three parts. On the lake bottom, it is cold and dark. Few animals live there. Near the surface float tiny **plankton**. Plankton are eaten by fish, like bass.

The busiest part of the lake is near the edge. Here plants grow. There are snails and insects, like water boatmen. Fish with slim bodies, like sunfish, move through the plants.

Ponds are smaller and shallower than lakes. They sometimes dry up. Water plants can grow anywhere in a pond. Ponds attract many animals. Some, like frogs, live in and out of the water. Frogs are **amphibians** (*am-fib-ee-ans*). The frogs arrive in spring and lay eggs in the water. When the young tadpoles hatch out, they must grow fast to become frogs before the pond dries up.

15

Life in wet lands

Swamps and marshes are areas of wet land. They can be near the coast, or inland. Their waters are still, or **stagnant**, and are slightly salty near the coast.

Marshes are open, grassy areas. Swamps are like flooded woods. They are both areas that people are not at home in. We have drained many wetland areas to make dry land.

▼ A green heron wading in a swamp in Florida, USA. The green heron is one of the smaller members of the heron family, and grows to about 40 cm in length. It dives into the water in search of prey.

Animals that live in these wet areas are quite at home. Many of the larger animals have **webbed feet**, to stop them sinking. Plants, too, have to cope with a watery life. Although the soil is rich, it is usually flooded.

Life in the mud

Marshes close to the sea are called **tidal marshes**. Here, many of the plants are rushes. Snails crawl up the rushes. Fiddler crabs dart about, eating as they go. The snails and crabs are eaten by terrapins and herons. Herons are wading birds with long legs and wide feet. Their feet stop them from sinking into the mud.

Ducks, geese and grebes are birds that feed on the grasses and reeds of freshwater marshes. Grebes are birds with feet like paddles. The **bills** of wading birds are all

Life in wet lands

▲ Mangrove swamps are found near the mouths of tropical rivers. There are millions of insects. Larger animals include frogs, proboscis monkeys, bats and birds, such as the kingfisher.

sorts of shapes. The shapes suit the way they feed. Many birds sift through mud. Others spear small animals.

There are many newts and toads. Muskrats and large **rodents**, called nutria, run around. Rodents are gnawing animals.

Plants with unusual shapes grow in swamps. Swamps are often noisy, due to the croaking of the bullfrogs. There are biting insects, like mosquitoes. Some swamp animals are dangerous. There are alligators and snakes. One snake, the water moccasin, drops from trees on to its prey.

Lungfish live in hot swamps. If the swamps dry up, the fish bury themselves in **cocoons** under the mud. They stay there until the swamps flood again.

Mangrove swamps

A mangrove is a tree which grows in swamps along **tropical** coasts. It has roots which stand above the water.

Little crabs live in the mud. Kingfishers, ibises and some frogs feed on the crabs. There are few **mammals** in mangrove swamps, but otters, monkeys and flying foxes can be found. These foxes are really bats.

Mudskippers are fish which live in the hot, steamy swamps. Mudskippers live in the mud above the water. They breathe air through **gills**, which they keep full of water. Mudskippers have to return to the water to feed and breed.

◀ Mudskippers live in water and on land. They grow up to 30 cm in length. They use their fins to climb out of the water and to move across the mud.

Grasslands of the north

Grasslands are large areas of dry land found on most **continents**. The grasslands lie between the forests and deserts. **Temperate** grasslands are cool. **Tropical** grasslands are hot. All grasslands are flat, or rolling **plains**. Little rain falls, which means that few trees can grow.

Grass is a tough plant with deep roots. Grass can survive if there is little rain. Animals which eat grass are called **grazers**. Most of the animals on grasslands are grazers. **Predators** attack the grazers. If the grass dries up, the grazers die. Then there is nothing left for the meat eaters. In the end, all the animals depend on the grass for survival.

Grasslands have few hiding places. Grazers either run fast, or burrow, to escape from their enemies.

Temperate grasslands are found in Central Europe, the Asian steppes and the North American prairies.

The prairies of North America

In the past, life on the prairies was unspoilt. The grass was eaten by bison (buffalo) and pronghorn. Pronghorns are swift runners, like antelope. Bison and pronghorn moved across the prairies, looking for fresh grass to eat. There were many prairie chickens. At the end of the **food chain** there were the meat eaters, like wolves and rattlesnakes.

▼ A herd of bison grazing in a North American nature reserve. Bison do not see well, but they do have a good sense of smell and good hearing. This is very useful if enemies are nearby.

Grasslands of the north

About 100 years ago, people moved to the prairies. They started to grow crops and rear cattle. They ploughed up the tall grass to grow wheat. Further south, the shorter grass plains were also ploughed up. They soon turned to dust. Most of the prairie was ruined. What happened to the wildlife? The wolves were poisoned. Now **coyotes** have taken their place. Millions of bison were shot. Bison are now protected by law.

The burrowers

Rodents called prairie dogs live under the ground. There, they can avoid predators and the cold. They have a well run life. Their living area is like an underground town. They have to go above ground to eat. Some keep guard, watching out for coyotes. Others pull out the weeds. This allows better plants to grow.

▲ Beneath the northern grasslands lies a secret world of tunnels. The prairie dog is one of many small animals that live underground. It is a relative of the squirrel. It gets its name because it barks rather like a dog.

▼ Pronghorns can run faster than horses, so they can escape from most predators. They are always on the alert, watching out for danger. Millions of pronghorn used to roam the prairies, but fewer are found today.

Grasslands of South America

Grasslands cover much of South America. The temperate grassland is called the pampas. It reaches across a vast area of land east of the Andes Mountains. The name comes from the grass which grows there, called pampas grass. It is a tall plant, like a reed. Much of this grass has been cut to make room for farming.

Burrowers and grazers

Pampas animals are mostly burrowers and grazers, like the prairie animals. The burrowers of the pampas include cavies and tuco-tucos. Cavies are wild guinea pigs. They have no tails, and look very like the pet guinea pig. Tuco-tucos have long teeth, which they use to dig with. The tuco-tuco's name comes from the noise it makes.

One pampas rodent, the viscacha, likes to clear the ground around its burrow. The viscacha then builds up mounds of earth, sticks and stones. These mounds are used as lookout posts.

Grazers include the pampas deer and a bird called the rhea. Sadly, the deer are now rare. Rheas look like small ostriches, and like them, they cannot fly. Rheas are fast runners, and roam the pampas in flocks.

▼ The pampas deer is one of the few large animals found on the South American grasslands. They graze in pairs or in small herds.

Grasslands of South America

▲ The long legs of the maned wolf help it to walk through tall grass. It hunts at night, often covering over 30 km in search of food. The maned wolf does not run very fast, so it hunts quietly, pouncing at the last moment.

Insect eaters

The insects of the grasslands include crickets, ants and **termites**. The insects are eaten by armadillos and giant anteaters. Armadillos have shells of tough, leathery plates. If they are attacked, they curl up in the same way that woodlice do. Giant armadillos, 1.5 m long, have 100 peg-like teeth for crunching insects.

Giant anteaters prefer to eat termites. The anteaters have long, strong claws which tear open termite nests. They have no teeth. Instead, they have a long snout with a sticky tongue which traps the insects. Giant anteaters can grow up to two metres in length.

Predators

Other hunters, or predators, hunt larger prey. The maned wolf eats rodents, birds, reptiles, insects or fruit. The maned wolf looks rather like a fox, but it is taller and has long legs. Sadly, the maned wolf is now rare. Another rare predator is the pampas fox. It has been hunted by humans, and now there are very few left.

Grasslands of Africa

Hot, dry grasslands, called **savanna**, cover much of Africa. Savannas are dotted with thorny trees and bushes. Rain only falls for a few weeks in the year.

Savannas are well known for their wildlife. Life is not easy for the animals. Camouflage is vital for some, strength or speed for others. Most of the animals can last a long time without water.

Tree and bush eaters

Trees, such as acacia, are food for many animals. There is a leaf eater for each layer of the tree. Let's take a lift up an acacia.

Near the ground, we see a dik-dik, a tiny antelope. Further up is an eland with curly horns. Higher up, is an elephant. The elephant's strong trunk tears the tree

Grasslands of Africa

to shreds. On the top floor is the tall giraffe. It searches among the thorns for tender leaves.

Another large animal, the black rhino, eats the savanna bushes.

Grazers

Most savanna grazers are **mammals** with hooves. One that is not is the ostrich, the largest and fastest running bird.

Many grazers follow the rule of safety in numbers. Herds of 10 000 or more wildebeeste, or 'wild oxen', and zebras roam together. Herds of gazelle also roam the savanna. Gazelles can run at speeds up to 65 kph. One type of gazelle, the springbok, escapes predators by leaping high into the air.

The African buffaloes are huge, weighing 800 kg. Buffaloes are dangerous when they are angry. If they are attacked by lions, the buffaloes can kill them.

Warthogs and white rhinos do not live in herds, but graze alone. Rhinos carry a bird, the cattle egret, on their back. The egret eats **ticks** from the rhino. The bird and the rhino help each other.

Predators

A well known hunter is the lion. The females do most of the hunting. They hunt in teams and kill large animals, like zebras and wildebeeste. Cheetahs are smaller than lions, but much faster. Cheetahs hunt alone. They hunt small prey, like gazelles.

All animals hate hyenas, because they steal food from them. Large packs of hyenas can drive a lion from its kill. Wild dogs have good teamwork when hunting. Although wild dogs are small, a few can bring down a zebra.

Other meat eaters are baboons, which eat rodents. There are also deadly snakes. Huge pythons squeeze their victims to death. The victims can be as large as an antelope! Some snakes, like puff adders, are poisonous.

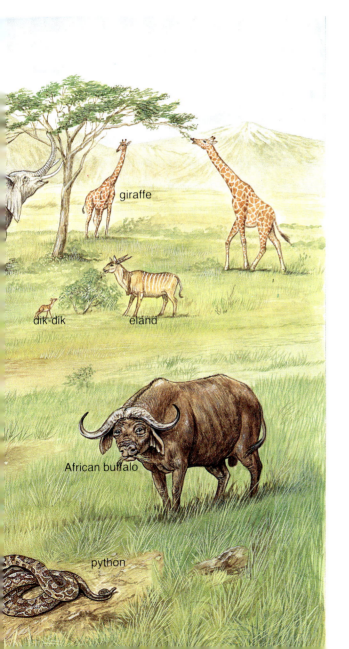

◀ The savanna grasslands of Africa are home to many different animals. Many of these are the biggest and best of their type. The African elephant is the largest of all land animals. The giraffe is the tallest. The cheetah is the fastest running animal. The ostrich is the tallest and fastest running bird. There are huge herds of wildebeeste and zebras. All these animals and many others have to share the hot, dry environment.

Grasslands of Australia

The savanna grasslands of Australia lie between vast areas of desert and tropical forests. They have less rain than the savanna of Africa. During the day it is very hot, and dry winds often blow.

Many of the mammals sleep through the heat of the day, and only come out at night. They are known as **nocturnal** animals.

Mammals with pouches

Australian mammals are not like most mammals. In most of the world, mammal babies grow inside the mother. In Australia the mammal baby grows outside the mother, in a pouch. Mammals with pouches are called **marsupials**.

▲ A frilled lizard putting on a display to frighten its enemies. Although its gaping mouth and wide collar makes it look rather frightening, the lizard is harmless.

Some marsupials do not look like other mammals. Kangaroos have large back legs which they use for jumping. The red kangaroo is the largest type. It is about 1.5 m tall. Kangaroos are grazers, and some can hop at speeds of up to 50 kph. Another grazer is the wombat. The wombat comes out at night to feed on grass, roots and bark. During the day it sleeps in its burrow.

Another animal that burrows is called the echidna, or spiny anteater. The echidna is one of the few mammals that lays eggs. The young echidna hatch in a pouch and then feed from the mother.

Few meat eating mammals are found. A few marsupial cats are found in the open savanna woodland, but they are more common in the forests. The Australian wild dog, the dingo, often hunts in packs.

◄ Red kangaroos in the Australian outback. When kangaroos are at rest, they use their tails for support. In the picture, you can see a young kangaroo in the mother's pouch.

Grasslands of Australia

Other animals

Although termites are tiny insects, they build mounds that can be taller than a person. Many thousands of termites live in these mounds. There are other insects, like grasshoppers. Swarms of grasshoppers cause a lot of damage to plants.

Lizards eat insects. Frilled lizards are like tiny dragons. Frilled lizards are only 20 cm long. When they are angry, they open their mouths and spread their frilly collars. This scares their enemies. Other **reptiles** include tiger snakes, which are like cobras.

Colourful birds live in the savanna. The budgerigar, always green in the wild, lives close to water holes. Bright blue mulga parrots are also found. The emu is an ugly bird with scruffy feathers. It is a large bird that does not fly. Wedge-tailed eagles, the largest eagles in the world, have wing spans of over two metres. They eat small marsupials.

▼ Water holes on the dry savanna are always busy. Predators know this and wait near water for their prey. This flock of budgerigars are flapping noisily to confuse any predators that might be nearby.

Animals in rain forests

Forests cover many parts of the Earth. They vary from cold pine forests to hot steamy jungles. Another name for jungle is **tropical rain forest**. There are rain forests in Asia, Africa, Australia and South America. Rain forests are found close to the Equator. The Equator is a circle which goes around the middle of the Earth. The lands close to the Equator are always hot and wet.

Rain forests are full of plants and tall trees which like hot climates. There are beautifully coloured flowers and twisting vines, as well as mosses and ferns.

Many animals are found at every layer of the forest. Bats and birds are at the top. Tree climbers are in the middle. Small animals are on the ground.

▼ A tropical rain forest can be divided into three layers. Different types of animal live in each layer. At ground level, small animals live in the thick undergrowth. A greater number of animals live in the trees of the middle layer. Above this, the taller trees spread out to form a roof, or canopy, of leaves and branches. The top layer is home for bats and birds.

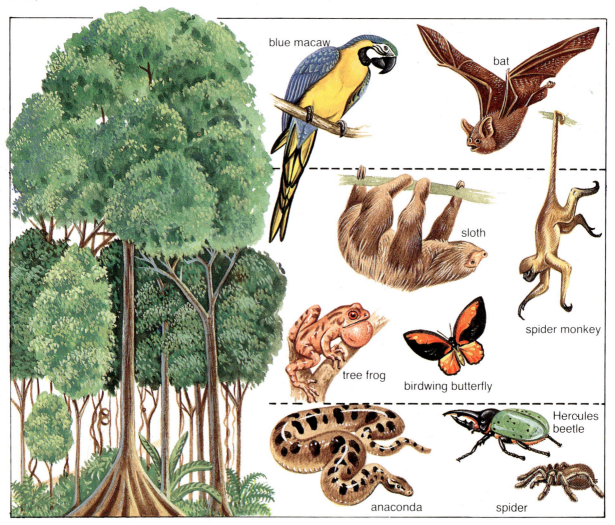

Animals in rain forests

▲ A young orang-utan hanging by its hands and feet. Orang-utans have a thin coat of red hair. Parts of their bodies are hairless and their grey skin can be seen. Orang-utans are found in the forests of Borneo and Sumatra.

Climbing animals

Animals that do not fly have to be good climbers. They need to climb to reach the fruit and flowers in the trees. They also need good eyesight. This helps them to leap from branch to branch.

One of the best known groups of climbers is the **primate** group. This group includes apes and monkeys. Apes and monkeys have better brains than most animals. They also have hands with thumbs. Their hands are useful tools which help them to grip branches. Some monkeys, like the spider monkey, use their tails as an extra arm.

Many primates are clever. Large red Asian apes, called orang-utans, know how to find food. They work out which trees have fruit by watching the movements of birds.

Other climbers include sloths and koalas. Sloths are slow moving plant eaters. They are only found in South America. Koalas live in Australian forests and have sharp claws.

Other animals

Rain forests are full of interesting animals. In South America there are huge insects like the 15 cm long Hercules beetle. There is also a spider which grows up to 25 cm across and feeds on small birds. In New Guinea there is a butterfly, called the birdwing, which has a wingspan of 30 cm.

Frogs like wet, warm, or **humid** places. Some are tiny and colourful. Many are poisonous. Tree frogs have sticky pads on their feet so they can cling to smooth tree trunks.

Reptiles are also found. Anacondas, large snakes up to 11 m long, strangle their prey. Other **predators** include members of the cat family. Bengal tigers are found in Asia, and jaguars in South America.

Animals in woodlands

The hot, wet rain forests are found in the **tropics**. The tropics are close to the Equator. Moving north or south of the tropics, the land gets cooler. These lands are called the **temperate zones**.

In the temperate zones, there are forests and woodlands. They are found in North America, Asia and Europe. They are not like rain forests. Rain forests are hot all year. Temperate woodlands have cold winters and hot summers. These changes through the year are known as the **seasons**.

The seasons have a strong effect on woodland life. Many trees drop their leaves before the winter. They do this to guard against the cold. In the spring, things start to grow again. Small bushes and plants burst into life. The plants have to grow quickly, before the leaves of the trees block out the sun.

▼ A red deer stag. Red deer are found in the woodlands of North America and Europe. The males, or stags, have bony antlers which drop off each spring. New antlers grow in the summer.

Animals in woodlands

Food all year round

In the growing seasons, animals eat the plants. Plant food includes buds, leaves, flowers, fruit and nuts. In the winter, there is little to eat. Some animals, like squirrels, store food for the winter. Others get as fat as they can, then rest during the winter. Their body fat keeps them alive.

Small **mammals** include mice, shrews and hedgehogs. They eat plants and insects. The small mammals are prey for badgers, racoons and foxes. These animals like meat, but they also eat plants.

In the past, bison and boar grazed in the woods. Today, few are found. People are the main reason for this. They chopped down the trees and shot the large animals. Black bear still survive in North American woods. The most common large animals are the deer.

▲ A selection of woodland mammals. The black bear and the racoon are found only in North America. The hedgehog and the European badger are found only in Europe. Squirrels and mice live in all woodlands.

Life in the trees

Trees support a lot of animal life. Look closely at a tree. You will see ants and beetles. Caterpillars move slowly, eating the leaves. Some insects, such as gall wasps, live in little red 'balloons', or **galls**, which they build on leaves.

Birds of many kinds can be found in woodland trees. Flycatchers are birds that eat insects. Their beaks have bristles which trap insects. Other birds, like cardinals, have short beaks for cracking nuts. Owls are meat eaters. Their beaks are curved and pointed for tearing flesh.

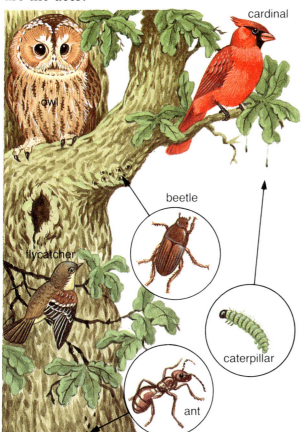

◀ An oak tree is home for thousands of small animals. These include beetles, caterpillars and ants. Birds include owls and flycatchers. Cardinals are found only in North America.

Animals in pine forests

Pine forests stretch across Canada, Alaska, northern Asia and Europe. They lie north of the temperate woodlands, among lakes and rivers. Summers are short and mild. Winters are long and harsh.

Pine trees can live through the cold. Their leaves are like tough needles. The trees do not bear flowers or fruit. Instead, **cones** protect the seeds. Trees that have cones are called **conifers**. They include fir, spruce and pine trees.

Most conifers are **evergreen**. This means that their leaves do not fall at once. Conifer forests are dark and shady all year. Ground plants hardly grow at all. The forest floor is thick with dead needles.

Warm coats

Some animals, like the moose and brown bear, are found right across the northern forests. All the mammals in the north have thick fur for warmth. Many of these animals, like the mink, sable and beaver, have been hunted for their fur.

Mink live by the water, eating fish and **rodents**. A much larger relative of the mink is the wolverine. It is a strong, fearless hunter. Other hunters include the wolf and the lynx. The lynx is a strong, stocky cat with ear tufts. The lynx has large feet to stop it from sinking into snow. Brown bears, including huge grizzlies, live here too.

Plant eaters include beavers and moose. Beavers are at home in water and have webbed feet. The moose is a large animal, up to two metres tall at the shoulder. Moose find little food in winter, and they have to eat the bark from trees.

Birds and insects

Few reptiles and amphibians live this far north. They have no fur or feathers to keep them warm.

There are fewer types of insects in pine forests than in woodlands. Insects that are found live in great numbers. Spruce bark beetles and wood wasps live in pine trees. The female beetles make holes in the tree trunks into which they lay their eggs. The young insects stay in the tree until they are adult. Wood wasps only lay eggs in dead, or dying trees.

Insects are food for birds like creepers and warblers. The most well known insect eaters are the woodpeckers. Their beaks cut tunnels into tree trunks. Then their long, sticky tongues reach into the tunnels and trap ants.

A bird called the crossbill has a scissor shaped beak. It uses its beak to open pine cones. Hunting birds include bald headed eagles, and fish eating ospreys.

▲ A moose with a calf. This calf is nearly one year old. Moose calves are born in May or June. They stay with their mother until she produces another calf. The moose is the largest of all deer.

◄ Brown bears are some of the largest meat eaters. The photographer took this picture from the safety of a tree. He may not have known that very hungry bears sometimes climb trees.

▲ The bald headed eagle of America. This is a famous bird of prey. It is skilled at swooping down to catch fish which come to the surface of lakes and rivers.

Life in the coldest places

Beyond the forests of the north lies the **tundra**. The tundra is the coldest land area of the north. The ground is frozen most of the time. During the short summer, the earth **thaws** a little. Plants then have a chance to grow in the boggy soil. The plants include heathers and grasses.

Beyond the tundra lies the Arctic Ocean and the North Pole. The Arctic is usually frozen solid. In summer, some of the ice breaks into moving chunks. The North Pole is always frozen.

At the opposite end of the world is the South Pole. The South Pole is on a large area of land called Antarctica. This land is covered with thick ice. Very few plants grow there.

The North

Plant eaters on the tundra include lemmings, musk-oxen and caribou. The other name for caribou is reindeer. Musk-oxen have long, shaggy coats for warmth. They are heavy animals, 1.5 m tall. Small animals, like lemmings, are food for weasels, arctic foxes and snowy owls. Wolves hunt the musk-oxen and caribou.

Polar bears live on the tundra during the summer. In winter, they live on the Arctic ice. There they can hunt seals. Seals and walruses live in and out of the water. Thick fat protects them from the cold. Seals and walruses are **sea mammals**. Other sea mammals are the whales. Unlike seals and walruses, whales always stay in water. White belugas and narwhals are Arctic whales. Narwhals have a long tusk which looks like a unicorn's horn. The tusk of a narwhal can reach three metres, over half the narwhal's total length.

▲ The polar bear is the biggest and strongest predator of the far north. It is seen here in the summer on land, where it searches for any type of food that it can find. During the winter, it lives on the Arctic ice and hunts seals. The male hunts alone, leaving the female to hunt with her cubs.

The South

Most of the animals which live in Antarctica are birds. There are few plants for them to eat. They must depend on the sea for their food. Many types of birds can be found living near the sea.

Life in the coldest places

One of the birds which nests in Antarctica is the albatross. Albatrosses spend most of their lives roaming the oceans. They are the largest living birds, with wing spans of three metres. Penguins are very different birds to the albatross. Penguins use their wings for swimming, not for flying. They are good divers, with torpedo shaped bodies. The largest penguins are the Emperor penguins. They are over 90 cm tall. The males use their bodies as nests. They stand over the eggs to protect them. Sometimes they stand in blizzards for weeks while the females search for food. When the females return, they take over from the males and feed the chicks.

Leopard seals eat penguins. Other seals are fish eaters, like Weddell seals. Crabeater seals eat tiny shrimps, called krill.

▲ A Weddell seal with pup. The Weddell seal is very clumsy on land, but in the water it is sleek and fast. It can dive to a depth of 600 m in its search for food.

▼ These Emperor penguins normally move on land by using their short legs. If alarmed, they move off by tobogganing on their bellies.

Animals that hibernate

Some animals find it hard to live in winter. The cold and lack of food are their main problems. Food supplies are hard to find. In winter, trees drop their leaves. Animals who like eating leaves have to eat the bark of the trees instead. Nut eaters have few problems. Nuts are easily stored for winter use.

If animals stop moving, they need very little food to keep alive. So, if food is lacking in winter, some animals **hibernate**. This means that they have a long sleep. Before sleeping, they eat as much as they can to get as fat as possible.

All mammals and birds can make their own heat. They are called **warm-blooded** animals. All other types of animals are **cold-blooded**. They cannot make their own heat. The weather controls their body heat. They like to live in warm places.

▲ A hibernating dormouse. This winter sleep lasts from late October until April. During this time the dormouse does not move and its breathing is very slow.

▼ A black bear hibernating. The bear does not sleep as heavily as the dormouse. The bear wakes from time to time, but even so it will not eat or drink for months.

Animals that hibernate

Warm-blooded sleepers

There is only one bird that hibernates. This is the poor-will, a little American bird. All other warm-blooded sleepers are mammals.

Some mammals sleep for short periods. From time to time, they wake up to feed. This is not deep hibernation. Bears, badgers and chipmunks behave in this way. Other mammals go into a deeper sleep. Their breathing and heart beat slow down. Also, their body heat drops. While they are in this deep sleep, their body fat is used to keep them alive. They do not wake until spring comes. Small mammals like dormice, hedgehogs and ground squirrels are deep sleepers. They often sleep curled up, to keep warm.

Cold-blooded sleepers

Frogs are cold-blooded. They do not hibernate only in winter. Cold-blooded animals are only active if they are warm. If there is a cold spell in summer, their bodies cool down. Then they have to rest. Some mountain frogs have to rest for eight months!

Frogs sleep under dead leaves, or in the mud at the bottom of ponds. Painted frogs and natterjack toads are examples of deep sleepers.

Reptiles which hibernate include wall lizards, pond turtles and small snakes called asps. Some asps live in the mountains of Europe. They rest in large groups. They make nests under the ground, beneath stones, or in a hollow tree.

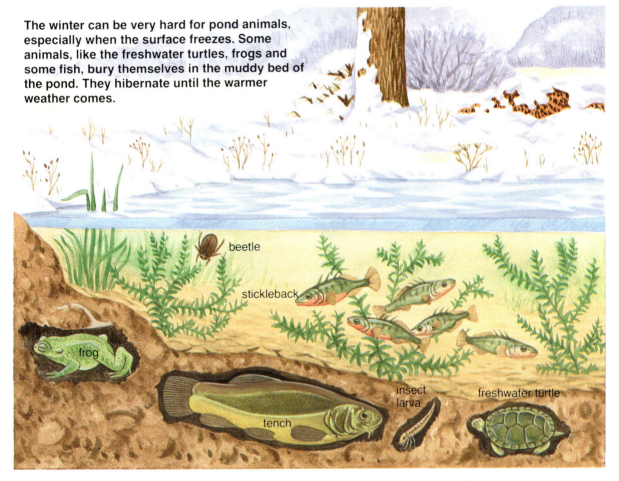

The winter can be very hard for pond animals, especially when the surface freezes. Some animals, like the freshwater turtles, frogs and some fish, bury themselves in the muddy bed of the pond. They hibernate until the warmer weather comes.

Mountain animals

The further up a mountain you go, the colder it gets. Also, the growing season gets shorter. Finally, a point comes where plants cannot grow at all.

Mountain life has many problems. Winds are strong. The high mountain air has little **oxygen**. Oxygen is a gas that all living things need. Both animal and plant life have to cope with steep, rocky slopes.

Most mountain plants have short stems. Plants with long stems could not stand the wind. Many mountain plants are shaped like spongy cushions, which helps to keep in warmth. Their flowers are brightly coloured to attract as many insects as possible in the short summer.

Most animals spend the summer in the high mountain meadows. As winter approaches, and their food becomes scarce, they go down to the lower valleys.

▼ The mountain goat spends most of its life high up in the mountains and rarely comes down to the meadows.

▲ Alpine choughs are found on the highest mountains in the world. They feed on insects and worms and live in flocks of about 20 birds.

Sturdy climbers

Plants often grow in places which are hard for animals to reach, like ledges. Mountain animals must be able to balance on ledges. European chamois (*sham-wa*) have rough hoof pads to stop them from slipping. Their American cousins are mountain goats, which have woolly, white coats.

Vicunas are rare animals which live in the Andes Mountains. Vicunas belong to the camel family. They are hunted for their soft red wool. Vicunas are found up to 6000 m. Their blood can hold more oxygen than normal blood. This helps vicunas to cope with the thin mountain air.

Pikas are small mountain mammals, like rabbits. Their feet have hairy soles, which grip well. They are like farmers. They collect grass and then dry it in the sun. It turns into hay, which they use for winter food.

Mountain hunters include pumas and snow leopards. Pumas are large cats. They used to be common in America, but now they are rare. Snow leopards live in Asia. They prey on wild goats.

Birds and insects

There are few flying insects in the mountains. They cannot cope with strong winds. Beetles, grasshoppers and low flying butterflies are found.

Mountain birds, like eagles and condors, are **soaring birds**. They float on the strong air currents which push up from below. Eagles kill small animals. Condors are huge American **carrion birds**. They eat dead meat, but never kill. Condors are very rare because many have been shot.

When Mount Everest was first climbed in 1953, men saw alpine choughs flying at over 8000 m. No other bird has been seen at this great height.

Desert animals

Many people think of deserts as being hot, dry, empty places. All deserts are dry, but not all of them are hot.

Clouds act like blankets. They keep the Earth warm at night and cool during the day. Without clouds in the sky, hot deserts quickly heat up during the day. Nights are cool. The daytime heat escapes quickly into the sky. This happens because there are few clouds.

It hardly ever rains in deserts, so plants have to last long periods without water. When it does rain, desert plants burst into life. They take in as much water as they can. Many desert plants have thick waxy leaves to stop water from escaping.

Heat, food and water

There are several ways that desert animals cope with the heat and lack of water. During the heat of the day, many small mammals keep cool by staying in their burrows. At dawn and dusk, mice, jerboas, kangaroo rats and other small animals come out in search of food.

The bodies of some animals are shaped to keep them cool. Fennec foxes and jack rabbits have huge ears. The ears pass the animals' body heat to the air, like radiators. This keeps the animals cool.

Some desert animals, like the kangaroo rat, never have to drink. All the water they

A herd of springbok. These animals live in the hot, dry regions of southern Africa. There used to be vast herds of springboks, but today they are becoming rare.

Desert animals

▲ The fennec fox is the smallest of all foxes. It lives in the dry lands of Africa. It feeds on lizards, insects and small rodents.

need comes from the food they eat. Their bodies do not sweat, so water is kept in for as long as possible.

Larger mammals, like camels, can go for long periods without drinking. When they find water, they drink vast amounts. The smaller oryxes, with long pointed horns, also rarely drink. They get water from the plants they eat.

Reptiles and insects

Many reptiles and insects are found in hot deserts. These animals like warm places. They do not lose much water through their dry skins.

One type of bug, called a coccid, covers itself with a waxy coat if no rain comes. It stays like this for many years. When rain eventually falls, the insect comes to life again.

Reptiles are at home in the desert. Lizards and snakes are a common sight, although they avoid the burning heat if they can. Some burrow in the sand. Sand boas and dune vipers are snakes that burrow. They are the same colour as sand, so they are hard to see. They prey on small desert animals.

▼ A sand diving lizard. This lizard wriggles through the sand like a snake and pushes itself along with its strong back legs. It searches for insects beneath the surface.

Animals of the night

Most people are active by day and sleep at night. In the wild, there are many animals that sleep during the day and are awake at night. These animals are called **nocturnal** animals.

Why do some animals live by night? In the desert, many animals sleep through the day because of the heat. They can move around at night without getting too hot. The night is safe for many animals. In **tropical rain forests**, insects and small frogs are safe from birds. Most birds sleep at night. Hunting animals also like to move at night. They move quietly, unseen, and creep up on others that are fast asleep.

On the prowl

Most cats, large and small, like to hunt by night. Like many night animals, cats have good night sight. In the dark, they can see six times more than people. The leopards of Asia and Africa are night prowlers. They hunt small antelopes called duikers. Jaguars, from South America, hunt small deer called pudus, which are only 30 cm tall. The only cat that does not hunt at night is the cheetah.

Another night prowler is the shy aardwolf, a member of the hyena family. Its favourite food is a type of termite which is active at night. The aardwolf's tongue is long and sticky so that it can lick up the termites.

Some animals **scavenge** at night. These animals include foxes, badgers and jackals. They search for scraps of food. This is easier than hunting live animals. Foxes and badgers sometimes raid dustbins.

Night senses

As well as having good sight, animals of the night need other **senses**. Good hearing is important. Owls have very good hearing. They can find their **prey** on the darkest night by listening. Smell is also useful. The aardwolf finds termites by smell. Kiwis, from New Zealand, hunt for worms by smell. Their nostrils are at the end of their long bills.

Bats are well known night animals. Bats are flying mammals. Their sight is not good. Instead, they find their way around in a very unusual way. If you shout in a large cave you will hear an **echo** of your voice. The sound of your voice bounces back off the walls. Bats have learnt to use echoes to find their way around. This is called **echolocation**.

▲ A European badger on the prowl at night. Badgers like to scavenge for food. They also hunt small animals like frogs, toads, snails and mice.

Animals of the night

▲ Owls are night hunters. Their soft feathers hardly make a sound as they fly through the air. Both their eyes face forward which means that owls rarely miss their prey as they swoop in for the kill.

▶ Bats flying in search of food. The picture shows how the wings are made of flaps of skin which are stretched over a framework of thin bones. The bones are like very long fingers.

Animals on the move

So far, we have looked at all sorts of **environments**. We have also looked at the animals that live in these places. Lions, for instance, live on the grasslands of Africa. Many animals do not stay in one place. They make long journeys, moving at certain times of the year. Their journeys are called **migrations**.

Why do animals migrate? There are a number of reasons. When the **seasons** change, the weather changes. If the weather becomes too cold, some animals move to warmer places. Other animals move when their food supply runs out. **Grazers**, for example, move to fresh grasslands. They will return after the grass has grown.

Many birds migrate to **breed**. Other animals, like some fish and turtles, also migrate to breed.

Long journeys

During the summer, caribou feed on the small plants of the **tundra**, in Alaska. As winter comes, the caribou gather in large herds to move south. The caribou herds always use the same routes. They travel 1000 km or more to find warmer grazing grounds.

In Africa, if there has been no rain, the savanna grasslands dry up. Animals such as zebra and gnus move long distances in search of fresh grass and water.

Small animals migrate too. Army ants march across forests, causing a lot of harm as they go. Some types of butterfly and moth migrate to warmer places. Monarch butterflies fly from Canada to Mexico to miss the winter. They move back north in the summer.

▼ A huge herd of wildebeeste and zebras crossing a river in Tanzania, Africa. The rainy season is over and the rivers and land will soon dry up. The animals are migrating westwards in search of fresh grazing land. They will return when the dry season is over and the grass has grown again.

Animals on the move

Record breakers

Nearly half the world's birds migrate. It is easy for them to escape winter, because they can fly. Birds which migrate include terns and plovers. The Arctic tern is a record breaker. It spends one summer in the Arctic. Then it flies over 18 000 km to spend another summer in Antarctica. Golden plovers fly from the northern tundra to the pampas of Argentina. On the trip, they can fly 800 km in one day.

Fish migrate too. Salmon are born in rivers, well upstream. When they are older, they swim to the oceans. They live in the oceans until it is time to breed. Then they return to the streams and rivers where they were born. How they find their way back to the right spot is still not known.

◀ These migrating cranes breed in the marshy areas of northern Europe and Asia. They are moving south as the winter approaches, in order to avoid the cold.

▼ Caribou on their long journey south. Caribou can stand the cold better than most animals. They move south to find food as well as to escape the cold.

Animals on islands

Islands can be any size, from a few hundred metres across, to hundreds of kilometres. Islands are land surrounded by water. Some islands are in the middle of lakes, or just off the coast. Others are in the middle of oceans.

The islands in the middle of oceans are a long way from the rest of the world. Some have no people on them. This means that animals can live on them without being disturbed. Only certain types of animal are found on these islands. Most land mammals and **amphibians** are missing. They cannot swim across the oceans to reach the islands. Many types of insect are not found. Reptiles also find these far off islands hard to reach. The most common island animals are birds.

▲ A small island crowded with gannets.

▼ Seabirds are usually the first animals to reach newly formed islands. Seagulls were among the first to arrive on Surtsey, a volcanic island off Iceland, which arose in 1963.

Animals on islands

A safe home

Birds flock to islands to breed. Some islands become very crowded. The bird nests almost touch each other. Gannets, gulls, boobies and terns are examples of birds that crowd on to islands to breed. There they are safe. How do these island birds find food? The answer is that most island birds are seabirds. Seabirds get their food from the sea.

The Galapagos Islands in the Pacific Ocean are a safe home for the animals that live there. Giant tortoises, 1.6 m long, are found there. Iguanas also live on the Galapagos Islands. Iguanas are like huge lizards, up to two metres long. Tortoises and iguanas are reptiles. If they had to compete with mammals for food on the islands, they would not be so successful.

▼ Relatives of this tuatara once lived all over the world. The few that are left live on a few islands off New Zealand. Tuatara feed on snails, insects and other small animals.

Some dangers

People do not live on **remote** islands. When people do settle on these islands, they upset the **native** animals that live there. People bring other animals with them, like dogs, cats, goats and even rats. These animals upset or kill the animals already living on the islands. Most island animals cannot fight back.

One type of island bird, the dodo, once lived on an island in the Indian Ocean, called Mauritius. The dodos could not fly, so they were easy to catch. By 1680, so many had been killed that no dodos were left. They are now **extinct**.

Today, we try to be more careful. Island animals are protected by law. Reptiles called tuataras are only found on islands off New Zealand. Tuataras look rather like clumsy lizards. They are protected, and have been saved from extinction. They have lived on Earth for over 200 million years.

Taming wild animals

When the first people hunted for food, they had to travel long distances. Later, people kept animals so they did not have to hunt. They gave the animals food. When the animals were fat, they killed them. This is how the first farm animals, known as cattle, were tamed. Cattle today rely on people. They could not live in the wild for very long.

People have kept animals for thousands of years. Animals that people keep are known as domestic animals. They are kept for many reasons. Some are kept for their milk, some are kept for their wool and some are killed for their meat. Other animals have been taught to help people. They have been used to carry people and goods for hundreds of years.

Animal helpers

Horses are animals that help people. They can carry a rider over 80 km in one day. Each horse has to be trained to obey a rider. Horses are quick to learn. They can also be trained to pull wagons and carts.

In rich countries, cars and trucks are now used to carry loads. There are still some places, like mountain trails, that cars and trucks cannot reach. There, animals are still used. In poorer countries, many animals are still used to carry heavy loads.

▼ The horse is a very valuable helper. Rounding up cattle on horseback is hard work, but rounding up cattle on foot would be a lot more difficult.

Taming wild animals

▲ Camels have been used for thousands of years to carry heavy loads over great distances. Although they are very useful, camels are bad tempered and need careful handling.

▼ Peregrine falcons are birds of prey which can be trained to help people hunt small animals.

Cars and trucks are much more costly to keep. In Asia, elephants are trained to lift heavy loads, like tree trunks.

Some birds can be tamed to help people. Falcons are birds that have been used to hunt rabbits for a long time. Pigeons can be trained to carry messages. They can fly long distances with a message.

Animals help **disabled** people. Small monkeys are trained to feed people who cannot use their hands. Dogs are other animals that are helpful. Sheep dogs are trained to round up sheep. Guide dogs are trained to help blind people. Other dogs are trained to help find criminals, or to stand guard.

Our smallest helpers include bees and silkworms. Silkworms are young insects that spin silk thread. We take the silk thread and then make clothes with it. Bees have given us honey and wax for thousands of years. The bees work very hard for us. All we do in return is to give them beehives to live in.

Wildlife in danger

There was life on Earth long before the first people lived. We know this from the study of rocks and **fossils**. The fossils tell us that many types of animals once lived which are no longer found. Some of these early animals, like the dinosaurs, are well known to us.

The study of rocks tells us that the Earth is always changing. For example, we know that places which are deserts today were once covered by sea. We also know that the weather on Earth has changed through the ages. If animals cannot cope with the changes on Earth, they die out, or become **extinct**. Scientists think that the dinosaurs died out because the Earth changed from being hot, to being cold. The dinosaurs could not cope with the changes. Other animals can cope with change. Many types of insect, found today, lived on Earth long before the dinosaurs.

Animals also die out because new animals enter their **habitat** and kill them. A famous island bird, the dodo, died out this way. It could not defend itself against the animals that people brought to its habitat.

▼ Leatherback turtles lay their eggs in nests which they dig in sandy beaches. Once the eggs are laid, the female returns to the sea. Local people dig the eggs up and sell them in the markets. The number of leatherbacks is getting less and less, because so many eggs are taken.

Wildlife in danger

▲ A Siberian white crane, one of the rarest birds in the world. Cranes used to live in much larger numbers. In recent times, many have been shot because of the damage they do to crops. Their nest sites have also been turned into farmland.

We are now aware that a lot of animal life is in danger. If a habitat is destroyed, animals that live there have to be moved to safety. Wildlife parks have been set up around the world to provide animals with safe homes.

There are some 350 types of bird in danger around the world. Many of these birds live on islands. One is the Galapagos hawk. These hawks are only found on the Galapagos Islands. Their lives were disturbed when people came to live on the islands. Many were shot and their food was eaten by other animals. Now the hawks are protected by law.

All around the world, groups of people now care for animals. It may be too late to save some of the animals in danger. We are beginning to understand that the world belongs to all animals, not just to us.

The dangerous human

The most dangerous animal of all is the human. We kill millions of animals each year for their meat or skins. We kill other animals because they simply cause a nuisance to us.

There are now strict laws about hunting. The tiger is an example of an animal that used to live in great numbers. People hunted the tiger so much that there are now very few tigers alive.

People have made rapid changes to the Earth. We have cleared forests for farming. We have built cities, factories and roads. This has left many animals with nowhere to live. All this activity has led to the world becoming spoilt. A lot of waste is produced from factories and cities. Some of the waste is poisonous, which puts wildlife in danger.

▼ Tigers once lived in jungles throughout Asia. Experts believe that there are less than 3000 tigers in the wild today. Although they are protected by law, hunters still kill them for their skins, which fetch high prices.

LIFE IN THE WATER
Keith Porter

Introduction

Life began in the water over 4500 million years ago. Life only appeared on the land 300 million years ago. There are still huge numbers of animals in the **oceans**, rivers and **lakes**. Many animals are still being discovered in the deepest parts of the oceans.

There are two main types of water. One type is **salt water**. The **seas** and oceans contain salt water. The other type of water is **fresh water**. The lakes, rivers and streams contain fresh water. Very few water animals live in both types of water.

Freshwater fish cannot cope with the salt. They would soon die if they were put in the sea. Most sea fish would die if they were put in a lake. A few sea fish can live where the sea meets a river.

What is the main difference between salt water and fresh water? Salt water contains many more **chemicals** than fresh water. One of the most common chemicals in salt water is salt. If you have ever swum in the sea you will know how salty the water tastes.

▼ There is just as much animal life to be found in the water as on the land. There is life at all depths. Most water animals live near the surface. In this picture, taken close to the surface of the Red Sea, there are plants, fish and simple types of animal which cling to the rocks.

Introduction

Many places to live

There are lots of different places to live in fresh water. In some places, like lakes, the water is still. In other places, like mountain streams, the water flows quickly. Each river and lake has its own type of water and is a home to many different types of plant. This great variety of water and plants has resulted in thousands of different freshwater animals.

The seas and oceans also vary. Some seas are warm and very salty. Other seas are cold and not so salty. Most oceans are very deep. The oceans change as they get deeper. These changes are called the **ocean layers**. Different animals are found at each layer. There are many thousands of different ocean animals.

▲ Strange animals live in the dark depths of the ocean. The bodies of many deep sea animals glow with tiny lights. Many deep sea animals look fierce, but few grow to more than 20 cm in length. Some are hunters, while others feed on food which drops from above.

▼ These tiny animals, called krill, are about five centimetres in length. Krill are eaten by fish, seals, whales and birds.

The comfort of the sea

The first animals that lived in the sea were very **simple**. They only had a single **cell**. They ate tiny floating plants. Many of the animals in the sea are still simple animals. The water helps to support their bodies, so they do not need hard **skeletons**. They can float about in any direction, eating the tiny plants that float in the sea.

Oceans and lakes never get as hot or as cold as the land does. They stay at a steady temperature for most of the time. Some lakes do freeze over in winter. Very few seas freeze. When the surface of the sea freezes over, the water beneath it is not too cold for the animal life.

The water is a more comfortable place to live than the land. The water supports an animal's body. The sea does not warm up or cool down as the land does. Animals have to be much tougher to live on the land.

The simplest animals

The first animals were tiny. Their bodies were made of a single cell. Scientists think that the first animals may have looked like some of the tiny animals today. These tiny animals are called **protozoa** (*pro-toe-zoa*), which means the 'first animals'. Over 50 000 different types of protozoa are known. All types are made from a single cell. They are so small that we must use a **microscope** to see them.

Protozoa are found in lakes and oceans where they feed mainly on other tiny animals. Some of the tiny animals which they feed on are really half animal, half plant. Like plants, they use sunlight to make some of their food. The protozoa are eaten by many larger animals.

The amoeba

Some of the simplest animals are large enough to be seen as tiny specks. One of these is called the **amoeba** (*a-me-ba*). The amoeba is found in **ponds** and lakes. The body of an amoeba is always changing shape. It moves by pushing out part of its body. It seems to flow along. Amoeba eat tiny plants. When they feed, they simply flow around their food. The food is eaten inside a 'bubble'. Amoeba increase their numbers by simply splitting into two halves. Each half makes a new animal.

▼ The shape of the tiny amoeba is always changing. This amoeba is feeding. Its body has trapped a piece of food by flowing round it.

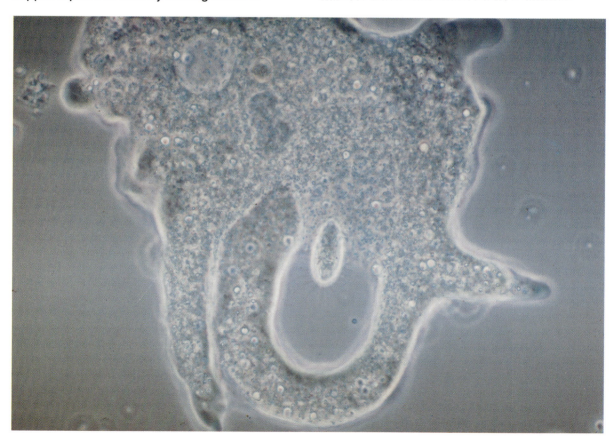

The simplest animals

Plankton

Millions of tiny specks of life float in water. They include plants, protozoa, and the young of larger animals. All these animals are known as **plankton**. Very young crabs, shrimps and **jellyfish** float amongst the plankton. These young look nothing like their parents. They are often flat or hairy. Their shapes help them to stay afloat. Much of the plankton is eaten by larger animals, like fish.

Sponges

Most animals have more than one cell. The simplest animals with many cells are called **sponges**. Most sponges live in the sea. A few live in fresh water. All sponges are cup-shaped. A few sponges have a type of skeleton made from a soft material. These strange skeletons are sold in the shops as bath sponges.

Most sponges live in large groups. The groups may cover rocks or even **shells** of larger animals. Sponges suck water in and out through holes in their bodies. The water contains their food.

◀ There are many different types of animal found in plankton. The tiny animals here are sea shrimps. Most animals in plankton can move but they all drift with the ocean currents.

▼ Sponges are very simple animals. Scientists once believed that sponges were plants.

Jellyfish and sea anemones

Some sea animals are well known to people who visit the seashore. **Jellyfish** and **sea anemones** are examples of animals that live near the shore. They both belong to the same group of animals. Jellyfish and sea anemones have mouths surrounded by arms, or **tentacles**. The tentacles are covered with tiny poisonous darts. The tentacles of some jellyfish give a nasty sting. The sting kills small animals which the jellyfish then eat.

Like most animals, jellyfish and sea anemones have **nerves**. Nerves pass messages between parts of the body. Most animals have a brain, so that they can think. Jellyfish and sea anemones do not have brains. Their nerves cross their bodies like a net.

▲ The thin tentacles of a jellyfish hang down from the bell in search of food. The inner 'tentacles' seen here are part of the mouth of the jellyfish.

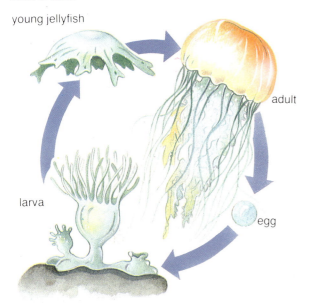

▲ After the larvae, or young jellyfish, are set free from the female, they attach themselves to rocks. They divide into groups and after several months they break away from each other and float free. Then they grow into adults.

Jellyfish

There are over 200 types of jellyfish. They live in oceans all over the world. Most jellyfish are about 30 cm across. The largest type is about two metres across. The body of a jellyfish is called the bell. The bell is the part that looks like jelly.

Jellyfish swim by pumping water in and out of the bell. They do this by using strong **muscles** around the bell. These muscles squeeze the bell in and out. If the muscles stop pumping, the jellyfish sinks.

The mouth and the tentacles are under the bell. Jellyfish have two types of tentacle. One type hangs down like a curtain from the edges of the bell. These tentacles have stinging cells. The other type hangs from the mouth. These tentacles help to take food into the mouth.

Jellyfish and sea anemones

Sea anemones

Most sea anemones live on rocks. They have a broad 'foot' which fixes them firmly to the rock. A few types of sea anemone burrow in sand or mud. Sea anemones get their name because they look like flowers. The brightly coloured 'flower' is a ring of tentacles. The mouth lies in the middle of these tentacles. The body of the sea anemone is full of muscles. If it is attacked, the sea anemone can pull in its tentacles.

Anemones also have tentacles with stinging cells. Tiny darts push poison into their **prey**. Once the prey is dead, it is pulled into the mouth. Most sea anemones eat small fish and shrimps.

A few types of sea anemone attach themselves to the shells of hermit crabs. The crab is not stung by the anemone. The anemone feeds on scraps of food left by the crab.

▲ Sea anemones do not move, so they need to wait patiently for their food to come to them. This anemone is feeding on a fish which has been poisoned by the anemone's tentacles.

▼ A group of sea anemones. Most of this group have their tentacles drawn inside their bodies. This could be because they were alarmed by the photographer.

Life in a shell

One of the largest groups of animals includes all the **molluscs**. Snails belong to the mollusc group. Most snails live in the sea. Mussels, clams and oysters are also molluscs.

All molluscs have a **shell**. Mollusc shells are made from a hard chalky material. Each mollusc makes its own shell. Some molluscs live inside **spiral** shells. Others live in a shell made in two halves.

Many molluscs feed on plants. They have a long, sharp 'tongue' which they use to tear off small pieces of plant. Other molluscs feed by trapping small pieces of food from the water.

The clam family

Clams have two halves to their shells. They live in sand or gravel. Each clam has a fat, strong 'foot' which it uses to pull itself down into the gravel. Clams feed by pushing two small tubes above the gravel. One tube sucks in sea water which passes down into the clam's shell. Small pieces of food are then taken from the water. Then the water is squirted out through the second tube. The giant clam does not burrow into sand or gravel. It lives on the sea bed. Giant clams can be as much as one metre across.

Snails and limpets

There are many types of snail. Periwinkles and whelks are types of sea snail. Pond and ramshorn snails are types of freshwater snail. All snails move slowly. They glide along on a wide, slimy foot.

A selection of animals with shells, found in different parts of the world.

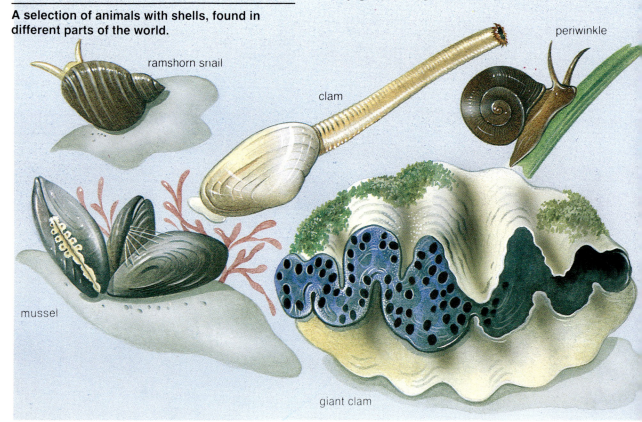

Life in a shell

As the snails grow, most of them add new twists to their shells. One type of sea snail is a limpet. Limpets have shells shaped like pyramids.

Oysters

All mollusc shells are smooth inside. The insides are often silvery in colour and some have bands of many colours. This is called **mother of pearl**. The oyster is a mollusc which uses mother of pearl to surround sand grains which get into its shell. The result is the precious pearl which some people wear as jewelry. Small pearls are also found inside molluscs called mussels.

Pearly nautiluses

The pearly nautilus is an unusual mollusc because, unlike other molluscs, it can float. This animal is a close relative of the octopus. The pearly nautilus also has tentacles, which it uses to catch food. Nautiluses swim by squirting water from a tube. This pushes them along quickly.

Barnacles

Some animals with shells are not molluscs. Barnacles are relatives of crabs and shrimps. They are small animals which look like limpets. When the tide comes in they open tiny doors in their shells. They use their feathery feet to feed. Their feet trap small pieces of food from the seawater.

Octopuses and squids

Octopuses, squids and their relatives are all molluscs. Most of them have their shells hidden inside their bodies. Some of them have lost all signs of a shell. A few, such as the nautiluses, still have a shell. Octopuses and squids have tentacles. They can swim quickly by squirting water from a tube. This pushes them along.

Octopuses

There are about 50 types of octopus. Most are quite small animals, about 15 cm long. A few can be as much as three metres across. All octopuses have eight tentacles. Each tentacle has suckers which can cling to their prey. Octopuses have two large eyes and a simple brain. If you look at an octopus, it seems to be all head and tentacles. The tentacles of octopuses help them to move, as well as to catch food.

Octopuses like to eat crabs. Their mouths have a strong pair of **jaws** that look rather like a parrot's beak. The jaws are used to tear pieces off the prey.

Octopuses can change colour to copy their background. If they sense danger, they have another trick. They can squirt a black 'ink'. This acts like a smoke screen. It hides the escape of the octopus from its enemy.

Squids

Squids spend their lives swimming about. They move slowly through the water by flapping two 'fins'. Squids can also move very quickly by squirting out jets of water.

Almost 400 types of squid are known. Most are only 20 cm or so long. The Atlantic giant squid reaches 16 m in length. They are the largest of all **invertebrates**. All squids have eight short arms and two long arms. The longer arms are used to catch fish. The fish is then pulled into the mouth. Squids have beak-like jaws, like octopuses.

◀ An octopus resting in shallow waters. The suckers on the tentacles can be seen clearly. Octopuses spend a lot of time in their dens where the female octopus lays hundreds of eggs. Unlike many sea animals, octopuses watch over their young.

Octopuses and squids

Some squids live in very deep oceans, where sunlight does not reach. Many squids have special 'lamps' over their bodies which produce a coloured light. These lamps might help them to signal to one another. Some types grow to over two metres in length.

Cuttlefish

Cuttlefish look rather like squids. They have ten arms which they use to catch shrimps. Most cuttlefish hunt at night. During the day they rest on the sea bed.

The shells of dead cuttlefish are called cuttlebones. They are often washed up on beaches. In the living animal the shell is inside its body. The holes in the cuttlebones are filled with gas. The gas helps the cuttlefish to float.

▲ A deep sea squid glows in the dark. All squids have arms which grow out from their heads.

▼ A cuttlefish searches for food on the sea bed. Cuttlefish can squirt ink, like the octopuses and squids, to escape from their enemies.

Crabs and their relatives

Crabs, lobsters and shrimps belong to the same group of animals. They are called the **crustaceans**. Most crustaceans live in the sea. A few types live in fresh water. All crabs and their relatives have five pairs of legs. They also have hard outer shells which protect their bodies.

Crabs

There are many types of crab. Most have four pairs of thin legs and a fifth pair of wide claws. Some crabs can swim. Their back legs are shaped like paddles. Most types of crab walk along sideways.

Many crabs use their front claws to catch small animals. They have sharp jaws which they use to bite pieces off their food. A few crabs, like the porcelain crab and the hermit crab, find tiny pieces of food in mud. They also eat dead animals.

▲ A red fiddler crab from the South Pacific. Fiddler crabs have one claw which is larger than the other. This is used for defence and to attract females.

▼ Hermit crabs live in the empty shells of sea snails. This hermit crab is sharing its home with several sea anemones. The sea anemones help to protect the crab from its enemies.

Crabs and their relatives

Crabs are common in rock pools near the shore. It is easy to see them in the pools when the tide goes out. If crabs stay out of the water too long, they will dry out and die. All crabs lay eggs. The newly hatched crabs live in the **plankton**. Crabs grow by changing their shells. They hide away while they break out of the old shells and wait for their new shells to harden.

Lobsters

Lobsters have longer bodies than crabs. Most lobsters live in holes on the sea bed. A few types burrow in the sand. The common lobster can grow up to 60 cm long. These giants weigh up to 22 kg.

▼ A member of the lobster family with very bright markings. Female lobsters produce eggs once every two years. The red-coloured eggs are carried on the outside of the body. Fishermen are not allowed to catch the lobsters which are carrying eggs.

Lobsters have huge claws, or **pincers**. These are used to catch other animals. Lobsters also bite pieces off their prey. Lobsters usually walk slowly. They can swim quickly backwards if they are attacked. They do this by using the flat 'paddles' on the ends of their bodies. Crayfish are just like lobsters, but they live in fresh water.

Shrimps and prawns

Shrimps and prawns are good swimmers. They do not have huge claws like crabs or lobsters. Shrimps and prawns have many small flattened legs along their bodies which they use like paddles, for swimming. They can also walk slowly on their five pairs of longer front legs.

Many shrimps can change colour so they match their background. This makes them very difficult to see. Shrimps and prawns feed on tiny specks of food which they pick up with two pairs of pincers.

Starfish and sea urchins

Starfish and sea urchins are unusual animals. Their bodies are divided into five equal parts. Each part is joined to the middle of the body. This gives many types their star shape.

All starfish and their relatives have a simple skeleton. This is made up of tiny bones. The starfish's skeleton is on the outside of its body and it can bend. The sea urchin's skeleton forms a hard, round shell on the outside of the body. The skeleton is covered in tiny **spines**. The spines give these animals the name of spiny-skinned animals, or **echinoderms** (*ekk-eye-no-derms*). Tiny tubes come out through holes in the skeleton. These are called **tube-feet** and they are used for walking.

▲ The cobalt starfish has five arms. The arms are used to help lever open the shells of molluscs.

▼ The underside of a seastar starfish showing the mouth and tube-feet.

Starfish and sea urchins

▲ Sea urchins are well protected animals. Their poisonous spines keep them safe from predators.

Starfish

There are over 1600 types of starfish. Some are brightly coloured, but most are a dull yellow. They live in seas all around the world. They are most common in the Indian and Pacific Oceans. Most are only 12–24 cm across. The largest starfish is 130 cm across. Starfish usually have five arms, but some types have up to 40 arms! Under each arm are dozens of tube-feet. These help the starfish to 'glide' over the sea bed.

Some starfish feed on molluscs or crabs. They use their tube-feet to grip their prey. The starfish feeds by pushing its stomach out through its mouth. The stomach is then pushed inside the prey's shell. After the prey is **digested**, the stomach is pulled back inside the starfish.

Starfish have another trick. If an enemy bites off one of a starfish's arms, the starfish can grow another one.

Sea urchins

Sea urchins do not have arms. Instead they look like round, prickly balls. They are found in seas all around the world. Some reach as much as 36 cm across. Most sea urchins are the size of tennis balls.

There are 800 types of sea urchin. All are covered in long, sharp spines. Their spines protect them. Some sea urchins have hollow spines. These can inject poison into any animal that touches them. They have tube-feet which stick out from between these spines. Some sea urchins have stinging tube-feet. Most sea urchins live on the sea bed and a few burrow into soft sand. They feed on seaweed or small pieces of food. A few eat small sponges or corals.

What is a fish?

Fish are not like other water animals. They have a bony skeleton inside their bodies. A stiff row of bones, called a **backbone**, runs along the back of the fish. Animals with backbones are called **vertebrates**. All reptiles, birds, **amphibians** and **mammals** are also vertebrates.

Fish are the only vertebrates to have **gills**. Animals with gills can breathe underwater. Most fish are covered in tough **scales**. Scales protect their soft bodies. All fish have **fins** which are used to help them swim. Some fins work like a ship's rudder and they steer the fish through the water.

There are over 22 000 types of fish. Fish come in all shapes and sizes. They live in seas, lakes and rivers all over the world. Some live in the deepest oceans, others are found in the smallest streams and ponds. Each type of fish has its own way of living. Some eat animals and some feed on plants.

Fish senses

Fish are very good at finding food. Many have good eyesight and a good sense of smell. Most fish can taste. They have tiny **taste buds** inside their mouths. Some fish make noises. Herring can make sounds which help to keep the groups, or **shoals**, together. A few catfish make groaning or creaking noises, which is their way of talking to each other.

Some fish have a special sense. They can make small **electric currents**. The electric currents work like a ship's **radar**. They tell

▼ The body of a typical fish. Much of the body is made up of muscles, which are used for swimming. Inside the body, the fish has a swim-bladder alongside its stomach. The swim-bladder helps to control the fish's depth in the water. The gills are used for breathing. The heart pumps blood around the body.

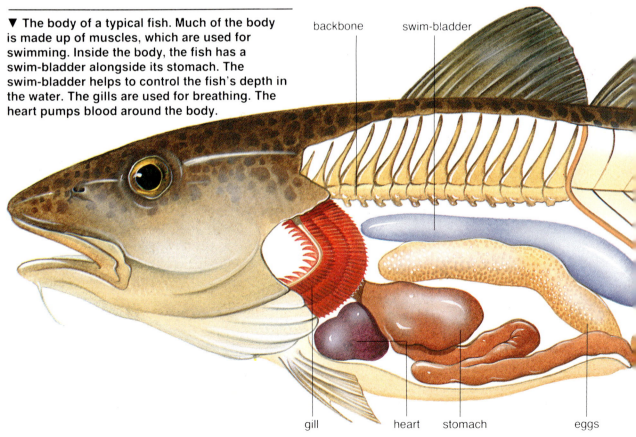

What is a fish?

the fish about its surroundings. Dogfish use this radar to find prey which might be hidden in the sand. Some fish that live in cloudy rivers use electric currents to 'see' through the murky water.

How fish breed

Almost all fish lay eggs. A cod usually lays two to three million eggs. These are squirted out over the sea bed. Then the eggs float up into the plankton. Here they hatch into baby fish called **fry**. The fry feed on tiny animals in the plankton. After three months the fry are about five centimetres long. Then they move back to the sea bed to feed with the adults. Very few of the millions of fry survive. Most will be eaten by other water animals or fish.

Some fish give birth to live young. They keep their eggs inside their body until the eggs are ready to hatch.

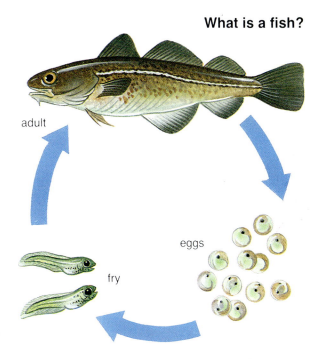

▲ The three stages in the life of a cod. Large numbers of eggs are laid which then float near the surface. The eggs hatch into fry. Most of the eggs and many of the fry are eaten by other animals. Some of the fry survive to grow into adults.

Breathing and moving

Most fish are active all the time. They often need to move quickly to escape from their enemies. They also have to dart to catch their food, especially if it is another fish. The bodies of fish are well suited to swimming. Most of their bodies are muscle. All fish have a good blood system. They have a heart which pumps the blood. Their muscles need a good blood supply, because they use up lots of energy.

How fish breathe

All active animals need a gas called **oxygen**. Most animals which live underwater can get oxygen from water. Fish do this by first sucking water into their mouths. Then the water is pumped from their mouths across their gills. The gills look like flaps of thin skin. Blood flows through the gills and picks up the oxygen from the water. The blood also passes waste gas back into the water. Most fish have a bony cover over the outside of their gills. This cover helps to pump the water by moving in and out.

Fish cannot breathe out of water. Their gills only work in water. A few fish, like the lungfish, have a type of **lung**. Lungs are used for breathing air. This helps these fish to live in water which has little oxygen. They can go to the surface and breathe air from above the water.

▼ Both air and water contain oxygen. Oxygen is important to animals because it helps to turn their food into energy. A fish breathes in a different way to a land animal. The gills of a fish need a steady flow of water to pass over them, so the fish receives as much oxygen as possible.

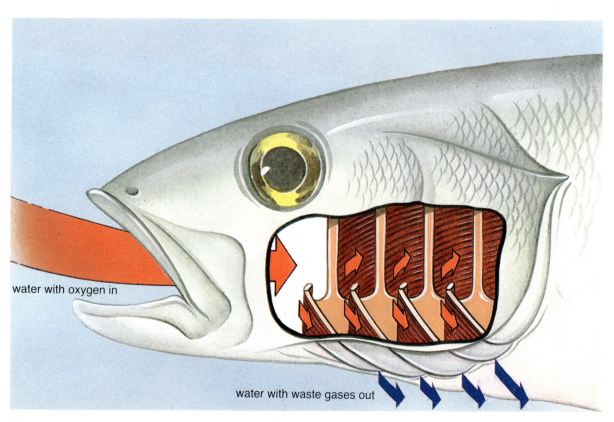

Breathing and moving

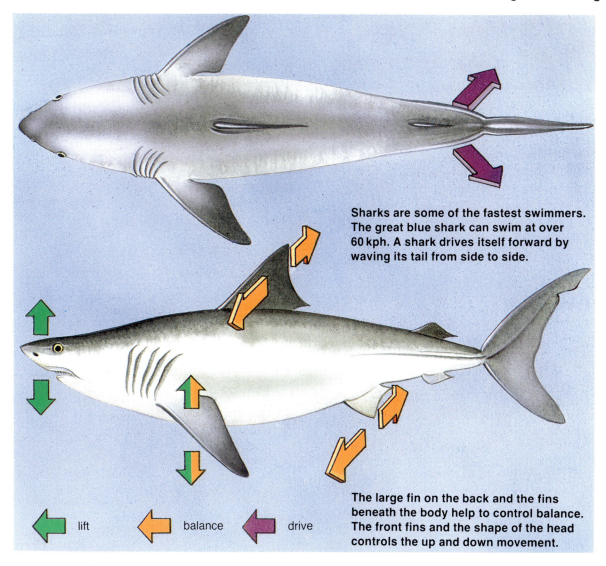

Sharks are some of the fastest swimmers. The great blue shark can swim at over 60 kph. A shark drives itself forward by waving its tail from side to side.

The large fin on the back and the fins beneath the body help to control balance. The front fins and the shape of the head controls the up and down movement.

lift   balance   drive

How fish move

Some fish are long and sleek which helps them to slice through the water. These long and sleek fish are often hunters. The fish's tail moves from side to side. This pushes the fish forward. The fins control the direction in which the fish swims. Not all fish use their tails for swimming. Flatfish and seahorses use side fins to move. Others wriggle like snakes or 'walk' on their fins.

Some fish have two kinds of muscle. One kind is used for slow, steady swimming. This muscle uses little energy. The second kind of muscle is used for quick darts. This kind uses lots of energy.

If people stop swimming, they tend to sink. Most fish do not sink if they stop swimming. They have an air bubble inside their bodies, called a **swim-bladder**. It can be blown up if the fish needs to come nearer the surface. Sharks do not have a swim-bladder. They sink if they stop swimming, so sharks must keep swimming all the time. Their fins help to lift them up as they move along.

Fish without jaws

There are three main sorts of fish. Most belong to the group called bony fish. The next largest group all have soft skeletons and include sharks and rays. The smallest group contains fish which have no **jaws**.

The jawless fish are very important to scientists. Jawless fish give clues as to how life first arose in the oceans. Jawless fish are simple vertebrates and look rather like eels.

The first fish

Fish are the oldest of all vertebrates. They swam in the oceans 450 million years ago. The first fish had no jaws. Many were covered with a tough armour. Most of the first fish would have fed on dead plants. They probably sucked this food up, since they could not bite.

These first fish were once very common. They ruled the seas and lakes for about 100 million years. Then, new fish appeared which had jaws. These fish also had teeth. These were hunters and jawless fish almost died out. They were no match for fish with jaws. Only 45 types of jawless fish are alive today. These jawless fish have lost the armour of their ancestors. Most jawless fish attach themselves to other fish by using their sucker-like mouths. Then they suck the blood from their prey. Some feed on the dead bodies of fish or animals.

Hagfish and lampreys

Hagfish are very simple animals. They look like fat, slimy worms. The largest hagfish are about 75 cm long. All hagfish live in the deep, cold oceans. They have no fins or eyes. Their mouths are like holes surrounded by six short 'tentacles'. Hagfish feed by using a strange tongue covered in horny teeth. They eat dead or dying fish. Hagfish lay eggs and when they hatch the young look like their parents.

◄ Fish appeared long before all other types of vertebrate. Some of the first fish had very strange shapes. Many had armoured bodies which stopped other fish from eating them. Their mouths sucked food into their bodies.

Fish without jaws

▲ A curled up Pacific hagfish showing the feelers around its mouth. The feelers are used to find food. They are very important because the hagfish are blind. Hagfish are most active after dark, when they search for weak or dying fish.

Lampreys look more like other fish. They have a few fins and a pair of eyes. This makes them look like eels. Some lampreys grow up to 90 cm long. Adult lampreys live in seas all over the world. Most types swim to fresh water to breed. They lay their eggs in gravel nests. The adults die after laying their eggs.

The eggs hatch into tiny **larvae**. The larvae make their homes in mud on the beds of streams. They stay there for several years. Lamprey larvae eat tiny plants in the mud. Once they are fully grown they swim to the sea. All adult lampreys feed on blood. Their mouths are large suckers with horny teeth. The teeth are used to break through the skin of a live fish. The fish starts to bleed and the blood is sucked in by the lamprey.

▶ The mouth of an Atlantic lamprey showing its horny teeth.

Lampreys are related to the hagfish but they differ in a number of ways. Lampreys have eyes while the hagfish have feelers. The feeding habits also vary. The lampreys feed on the blood of living fish. Hagfish eat crustaceans and fish.

Sharks and rays

Sharks and rays developed from the first fish. They are different from other fish because their skeletons are made of a rubbery material called **cartilage**. This is similar to **bone**, but not as hard. Sharks and rays have scaly skins. Each scale has a tiny 'tooth' which makes the skin very rough.

Sharks

There are about 250 types of shark. Most sharks live in the warm oceans. A few live in the cold Arctic seas. Others swim up large rivers. Sharks come in all shapes and sizes. Most sharks are less than one metre long. The largest fish in the world is a shark. This is the whale shark, which grows to 18.5 m in length. This huge fish feeds on the tiny animals in the plankton.

Most sharks have strong jaws. They need these for eating other animals. Most sharks eat other fish. Some live on **molluscs** and a few eat only turtles. The shark's mouth is under its head. The jaws carry rows of sharp teeth. The outside row of teeth is the oldest. As a tooth breaks off, a tooth from the next row replaces it. Shark's teeth are always growing.

All sharks find their food by smell. Some can smell blood 500 m away. Many people are terrified of sharks but very few sharks attack people. Most attacks on people are made by the great white shark. Other killers include tiger sharks and hammerheads. These fierce sharks usually eat large fish.

▼ The deadly tiger shark grows to about 5.5 m in length. This shark attacks anything that moves.

Sharks and rays

◀ The bonnet shark is a type of hammerhead shark. It grows to 1.5 m in length. Hammerheads like to prowl in warm seas in search of trails of blood. They follow the trails to find the source, which may be a wounded fish.

Rays

All rays have flat bodies. Over 350 types of ray are known. They include stingrays, sawfish and manta rays. Most rays live on the sea bed.

Rays have long, thin tails. Their eyes are on the top of their heads. Their mouths are under their heads. The smallest rays are only about 20 cm long. The largest rays, the manta rays, can be up to 6.2 m across.

The 'wings' of rays are really fins. These are used for swimming. The eagle and manta rays flap these fins. They seem to fly through the water, like strange birds.

Rays that live on the sea bed eat shrimps and molluscs. Other rays eat fish. Electric rays can produce **electric shocks**. They may use these to keep enemies away. Stingrays have tails with poisonous spines. These are used in defence.

◀ An electric ray glides through the water. Electric rays can grow up to two metres in length. These types of ray produce a powerful electric shock which stuns their prey. The ray waits on the sea bed until a fish passes overhead. Then the ray quickly grabs the prey and stuns it.

Bony fish

Most of the world's fish belong to one group. They are called the bony fish because their skeletons are made of bone. They are the most successful of all water animals. Over 20 000 types are known. Bony fish are found in fresh water and in salt water. Over half of them live in the oceans, while the rest live in lakes, rivers and streams. A few even live in water in underground caves.

▲ This adult French angelfish is one of a family which includes some 150 types. All angelfish have thin bodies with graceful shapes. The young French angelfish looks different from the adult. It has black and yellow stripes.

Different shapes

Bony fish are usually one of four shapes. Most bony fish are long and rounded. These types live in open water. Some types, like the angelfish, are flattened from side to side. They live among the water weeds. Their shape helps them to swim between the plants. Other types, like plaice, are flattened from top to bottom. These flat fish live on the sea bed. A few bony fish, like eels, are very long and thin. Their shape helps them to swim into small holes.

Some bony fish are strange shapes. The seahorse does not look like a normal fish. Its shape helps it to hide among the seaweed. The flying fish have a strange way of moving. They jump out of the water at over 60 kph and then use their wing-like fins to glide through the air.

▲ Seahorses are common in the shallow waters of tropical seas. This seahorse lives in the warm waters of the Gulf of Mexico. Seahorses swim very slowly in an upright position. When they are at rest their long tails grip on to plants.

Bony fish

Size and food

Bony fish come in many sizes. The largest bony fish, the oarfish, is long and thin and can grow to 7.5 m in length. The shortest bony fish is the dwarf goby. It is only nine millimetres long. Most bony fish are less than 40 cm long. Some can change their size very quickly. The puffer fish can suck air or water into its body to make it puff up like a balloon.

Each type of fish eats different food. Some fish have very wide mouths which scoop up the tiniest animals as they swim along. Other types eat larger animals and have strong jaws with sharp teeth. Lots of fish eat molluscs and crabs. Some of these types have wide, bony plates in their mouths. These plates help to crush the shellfish and the crabs.

The Coelacanth

Some fish are known only from their remains, or **fossils**, found in rocks. One such fish is called the Coelacanth (*seal-a-canth*). The Coelacanth was thought to have died out 70 million years ago. Then, in 1938, a live Coelacanth was caught in the sea near South Africa and several have been caught since. The first vertebrates to come on to the land may have looked like the Coelacanth.

▼ The Coelacanth has not changed shape for millions of years. The study of the Coelacanth can help scientists to understand how the first animals lived. The Coelacanth has a heavy body which grows to 1.2 m in length. It feeds on other fish and lives in the deep waters of rocky areas. Their fins are unusual, as they are thicker than those of other fish.

Protection from enemies

Fish have many enemies, so they need to protect themselves. Some fish use **camouflage**, so that they are difficult to see. The colour or shape of the fish blends in with its surroundings. Other fish are very fast swimmers, so they can escape from their enemies.

A few fish are armed with deadly weapons. The scorpion fish has poisonous spines which contain a deadly poison, or **venom**. Many types of ray have poisonous spines on their tails. The rays use these to attack enemies.

Hiding from enemies

Plaice are flatfish which live on the sea bed. Their body patterns make them very difficult to see. Flatfish cannot swim very quickly, so their disguise is very important. Some flatfish can quickly change colour to match the sea bed where they are resting.

Most fish which live in open water have similar colouring. They look dark from above and silvery from below. This helps them to hide from their enemies. Seen from above, their dark colour blends in with the deep, dark sea. From below, their silvery colour matches the light sky. Some fish use stripes to break up their outlines. The angelfish has black and white stripes. These stripes help the fish to hide amongst the weeds.

Strange shapes

Some fish are very strange shapes. The pipefish are perhaps the most strange. Pipefish like to live amongst the seaweed. Many of these fish have long strands, like leaves, on their bodies. This makes them look just like the seaweed. The anglerfish is another fish that has strands of loose skin for a disguise.

▼ This flounder has excellent camouflage, like many types of flatfish. The camouflage has two uses. Firstly, the fish's enemies do not see it. Secondly, the flounder can wait unseen for its prey to come close.

Protection from enemies

▲ A rock covered with weed or is it a fish? This anglerfish is another fish which is not easy to see. It will snap up any small fish which comes near.

Fish with armour

A few fish are covered in armour. This makes it difficult for other fish to eat them. The trunkfish, or boxfish, have a hard outer 'shell'. The shell is made of special bony scales. This stiff suit of armour makes swimming very difficult, so these fish can only move very slowly.

Porcupine fish have a strange way of defending themselves. Their bodies are covered in sharp spines. If porcupine fish are attacked, they puff out their bodies. The spines then stick straight out, which makes them look like porcupines.

The electric eel has a very good defence. The eel can produce a powerful electric shock. This shock stuns the largest of fish. Other fish can make bright flashes of light. These flashes frighten off their enemies.

▲ This porcupine fish has been alarmed. It has puffed up its body. The spines will keep most predators away. The porcupine fish looks like an ordinary fish when it is relaxed.

Ocean layers

Much of the Earth is covered by salt water. Oceans make up the largest areas. Seas are shallower and smaller than oceans. There are four oceans and twenty five seas. Oceans are very deep. The deepest oceans reach over 10 000 m in depth. Seas are rarely deeper than 200 m. All the oceans and seas run into one another. Winds and **currents** help to mix the seawater, which is never still. Some parts of this great mass of water are always warmer or more salty than others. These differences affect the animals which live in seawater.

surface layer

food sinks to ocean floor

Life in the oceans can be compared with life on land. There are plants, plant eaters, scavengers and predators.

ocean floor

Ocean layers

The different layers

Seas and oceans can be divided into layers. Most life exists in the surface layer, which reaches a depth of about 50m. The surface layer is where plants grow. Plants need sunlight to grow, and the sunlight does not reach more than 50m down. The sun also warms the surface layer.

Deeper down, the sea is always dark and cold. Only a few fish and squids live in these dark waters. Conditions are not easy for life deep down. Animals that live in deep water have to be able to stand the **pressure** of the water. Water pressure is the weight of the water which presses down from the surface. The further down you swim, the more water there is above you, and the water pressure becomes greater.

Fish which swim in the surface waters cannot stand the water pressure deep down. If they were taken to the ocean bed, they would be squashed.

A food chain

All life in the oceans depends on plants. Plants use sunlight to grow. Some animals live by eating these plants. This means that they can only live where plants grow. The plant eating animals are in turn eaten by larger animals. These larger animals are **predators**. They usually have sharp teeth and most live in the surface waters where the plant eaters swim. All these animals are part of a **food chain**. They depend on each other for food.

Some ocean animals eat dead animals and plants. They are called **scavengers**. Many others eat the tiny bodies of dead plankton. They are called **particle feeders**. Only scavengers, particle feeders and a few predators can live deep in the oceans because no plants grow at these depths. They all depend on food from the surface layers. The bodies of dead animals are always sinking to the sea bed.

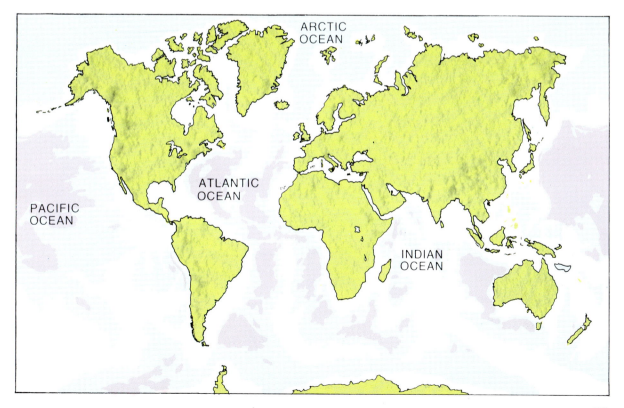

Life near the coast

The seas near the coasts are usually shallow. This means that light can reach down to the sea bed. Shallow seas are also quite warm. The light and warmth provide good conditions for sea plants to grow. These plants in turn provide lots of food for animals.

The sea bed

There are many types of sea bed. Some are sandy, others are rocky. Each type of sea bed has its own special animals and plants. Most plants prefer clear, shallow seawater. Many animals like to live at certain depths. Sea urchins, for example, cannot live below a depth of 10 m.

Almost every part of a shallow sea bed is full of life. The rocks and plants are covered in tiny animals. Sponges form living 'crusts' over the rocks. Tiny sea fans and sea squirts also cling to the rocks.

▲ A small shoal of bream in the Mediterranean Sea.

▶ A well camouflaged plaice on the sea bed.

Life near the coast

▲ A brightly coloured wrasse from the Red Sea. There are 500 types of wrasse, most of which live in warm waters.

The plants are eaten by snails. Other molluscs burrow in the sand or mud. They share their home with bristle worms, peacock worms and fan worms. Hungry fish roam across the sea bed. Some of these fish feed on the plants. Flounders and other fish join the crabs in the search for a meal.

Many fish live right on the sea bed. The rays and skates catch fish or crabs hidden in the sand. Plaice, flounders and halibut live on sandy sea beds. They are all flatfish, but plaice and their relatives begin as normal shaped fish. As a flatfish grows, its head twists around. Both eyes then come onto one side of its body. The side of the body with the eyes becomes the top half of the fish. The flatfish soon move to live on the sea bed. They lie on their eyeless side, so both eyes face towards the surface.

Fish in shallow waters

Huge numbers of fish live in shallow waters. These fish feed on many things. Gobies and wrasse live near the sea bed. They eat snails or small shrimps. Herring swim about in shoals. They eat tiny animals in the plankton. Bass eat other fish or crabs. Fish such as blennies like very shallow water. Blennies are often found in rock pools. Other fish live around shipwrecks or among beds of seaweed. Many other fish, such as cod, move to shallow water to breed. Their young find lots to eat in the plankton. Once the young cod have grown they move out to deeper water.

Coral reefs

A **coral** is a small animal. Corals look rather like sea anemones. Each coral has a simple body with tentacles. Unlike sea anemones, corals live in stony tubes. These tubes are made from a hard kind of chalk.

Corals live close together. They join up to make large areas of hard tubes. These tubes remain when the animals die. They form a type of rock which is often called coral.

Corals are found only in warm seas. Their skin contains tiny plants which help the corals to make their hard tubes. The tiny plants need sunlight to do this, so corals can only live in shallow water. Living corals grow on top of the dead ones. Over thousands of years they can build up to form underwater 'mountains' called **coral reefs**.

▲ There are many types of coral. This is a colony of soft coral. Soft corals have spongy skeletons which grow together to look like underwater bushes.

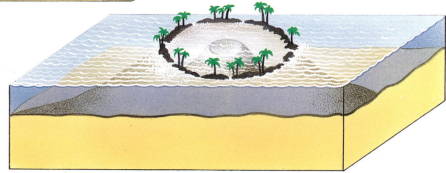

▶ When a volcanic island appears in a warm sea, a coral reef may grow around its edge. The volcano may then sink below the surface of the sea. This leaves a ring-shaped coral island, or atoll.

Coral reefs

Coral reefs grow near to the shore. Long reefs can form along stretches of coast. They are called **barrier reefs**. Islands can be surrounded by coral reefs. These are called **fringe reefs**. Some islands are made entirely out of coral. They are called **atolls**.

Swarming with life

Coral reefs swarm with life. Thousands of types of animal live there. Most of these animals are only found on coral reefs. A reef provides lots of places to live. There are underwater cliffs, caves and even 'forests'. Each place is a home for a different animal. The corals themselves come in many shapes. Some are rounded, like balls. Others look like deer antlers or organ pipes!

During the day the corals look dead. The tiny coral animals hide away in their tubes. At night, they push out their tentacles. The tentacles catch plankton or pieces of food in the water.

Many coral reefs are brightly coloured. Blue and yellow sea slugs can be seen, as well as red and white starfish. There are hundreds of small fish in all shapes and sizes. The colours of many fish help them to hide among the corals. The bright butterfly fish is difficult to see on the reef. Other fish have strange shapes. The parrot fish has a 'beak'. It uses its beak to scrape plants off the rocks.

Reefs in danger

Coral reefs do not last for ever. Sometimes they die if the sea bed sinks. This happens as rocks move deep in the Earth. The water soon gets too deep for light to reach down to the coral. Some coral reefs are destroyed by other animals. Many worms, molluscs and fish eat coral. A type of starfish, called the crown of thorns, has eaten away huge areas of coral reef, including large parts of the Great Barrier Reef off Australia.

▶ A coral reef is home to many animals. Sea anemones trap small fish with their stinging tentacles. The clown fish is the only fish which is safe from the sting of the sea anemone. The orange head of a clown fish can just be seen amongst the tentacles. The clown fish helps the anemone. It keeps the anemone clean by eating the small pieces of food which get trapped between the tentacles.

Deep sea animals

The deep oceans are dark and cold. No plants survive in such places, so no plant eaters are found. Some deep sea animals eat other animals. Many feed on the dead animals that fall from the surface layers.

We know very little about deep sea animals. Some are only known from photographs taken on the ocean floor.

The ocean floor is often 5000 m down and is usually covered in mud. This is where many of the deep sea animals live. Some feed on the mud itself, which is rich in dead bodies. Worms and molluscs eat tiny pieces of food in the mud. One deep sea animal, called the sea-lily, looks like a starfish on a stalk. The sea-lily's arms catch small pieces of food.

Gulpers and swallowers

Deep sea fish are very different to other types of fish. Most are coloured red or black. A few are clear, like glass. Almost all deep sea fish have huge, gaping mouths and lots of teeth. The deep sea viperfish has a mouth like a sabre-toothed tiger. Its huge teeth help to hold its prey. Food can be scarce in deep oceans and every meal counts, so the deep sea fish have stomachs which can stretch. This allows them to swallow fish as large as themselves.

▶ A lantern fish glowing in the dark. Most deep sea fish spend all their lives deep down on the sea bed. Lantern fish are unusual because on dark, moonless nights they rise up to the surface in search of food.

Glowing in the dark

The deep oceans are not totally dark. Some animals can make their own light. Many fish and other animals have tiny lanterns. The lantern-fish has rows of tiny lights along its body. Most have greenish 'lanterns'. Some have yellow or even red lights. On dark nights, unlike most deep sea fish, lantern-fish swim to the surface to feed.

Deep sea hatchet fish have lights all over their bodies. These lights attract their prey. Deep sea anglerfish also use light to catch their prey. They have glowing '**lures**' which dangle over their mouths and attract their prey.

▶ The deep sea anglerfish attract their prey with glowing lures. They can swallow fish almost as big as themselves. They have sharp teeth which stop their prey from escaping. Anglerfish have been found at depths of 3500 m.

Deep sea animals

85

The long journeys

Many animals make long journeys during their lives. Some animals make only one journey. Other animals move long distances every year. This is called **migration**. Birds, like swallows, migrate to avoid cold winters. Land animals, like zebra, migrate to avoid dry weather. These animals move every year.

Sea animals migrate too. Whales, turtles and many fish migrate. Although these animals can feed in many parts of the oceans, most of them breed only in certain places. The adult turtles and fish return to these places to lay their eggs. Some swim great distances to breed.

The Atlantic salmon

Adult salmon live in the sea. They migrate up rivers to lay their eggs. The Atlantic salmon may make this journey three or four times in their lives. The adult salmon swim up rivers in the autumn. They return to the same river which they were born in. The salmon do not feed while they are in the rivers. The female salmon scrapes a nest out of the gravel. Then she lays thousands of eggs in the nest. After laying the eggs, she covers them with gravel.

The baby salmon are called **parr**. Parr live in fresh water for up to three years. As they grow, they move further down the river. When they are 10 cm long they swim to the sea. Once they move to the sea they are called **smolts**. Smolts eat shrimps and smaller fish. The smolts grow quickly. Many feed in the cold seas near Greenland. They soon reach 70 cm long and become adults. After one to four years the adult salmon migrate back up the rivers to breed.

▼ A group of Atlantic salmon swimming up a river to breed. Salmon prefer to breed in fast flowing rivers, where there is plenty of oxygen.

The long journeys

▲ An Atlantic eel in a flooded meadow. In the past, people did not know where eels were born. Some people believed a story which said that the eels grew from plants which fell into the water. At last, a scientist discovered that the eels came from the Sargasso Sea.

▼ The migration routes of the Atlantic eels.

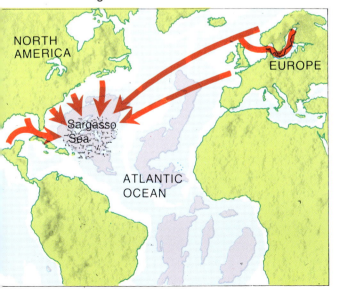

The Atlantic eel

Unlike salmon, adult eels live in fresh water and breed in the sea. Adult eels live in the rivers of Europe and North America. Their journey starts when the fully grown eels swim down rivers to the sea. Eels that live in ponds sometimes have to squirm overland to reach nearby rivers. All the eels travel to the same part of the Atlantic Ocean to breed. It is called the Sargasso Sea. All adult eels die after laying eggs.

The baby eels are a type of larva. They look like long, clear leaves. These tiny larvae float in the sea. They are carried along by the ocean **currents**. The baby eels drift for one to three years in the sea. Most of the young eels reach the coasts of Europe or North America. Where the rivers meet the sea, the young eels change shape. They are then called glass eels, or **elvers**. The elvers swim up rivers to become adult eels. After several years the adults return to the sea.

87

Life in fresh water

Many sea animals have relatives in fresh water. There are sponges, molluscs, shrimps and even types of jellyfish in fresh water. Some types of animal are more common in fresh water than in the sea. For example, lots of types of insect live in fresh water. Very few live in the sea.

Freshwater animals are different from their relatives in the sea. Freshwater animals have to cope with many different conditions. For example, the water in streams and rivers can move very fast after a lot of rain. Pond animals may find that their ponds dry out in summer.

▲ Snails belong to the mollusc group. The pond snail is a common freshwater animal. This snail has to come to the surface to breathe.

The smallest animals

Millions of tiny plants and animals live in fresh water, just as in the sea. The tiny plants use sunlight to grow. The tiny animals eat these plants. They, in turn, become a meal for fish, insects and birds.

Many animals in plankton are too small to see. They include protozoa, water fleas and insect larvae. None of these animals have a backbone. They are all invertebrates. Sponges, molluscs and shrimps are also invertebrates.

Many of the small freshwater animals live in mud or on stones. Snails are common in fresh water. They eat pieces of plant leaves. Many types of shrimp live under stones. They eat pieces of dead animals and plants.

A relative of the sea anemone can be found in some ponds. This is called the hydra. Hydras have simple bodies which are green or brown. On top of their bodies are some tentacles. The tentacles are armed with tiny stinging darts. These are used to kill the tiny animals which the hydras eat.

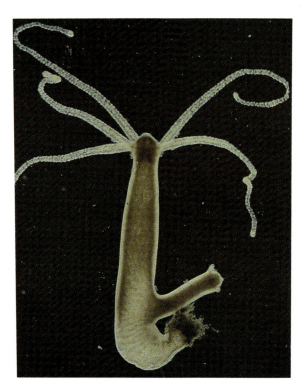

▲ A hydra grows to about 1 cm in length. Hydras breed by growing 'buds' which break away to form new hydras. A bud is growing on this hydra, to the bottom right of the picture.

Life in fresh water

Breathing

All animals must breathe. They need the gas called oxygen. Oxygen is used to produce energy from food. Small water animals can 'soak' up enough oxygen from the water. Fish, shrimps and others use gills to breathe with.

Some freshwater animals do not have gills. They must come to the surface to breathe air. Most adult insects breathe air. Some water insects carry bubbles of air with them, so they can breathe when they are underwater. Others suck air from hollow plant stems by using a special tube.

▼ A water beetle carrying a bubble of air. Water beetles feed on tiny animals and young fish.

Streams and ponds

Some animals live in fast moving streams. These animals have to cling very tightly to rocks and stones. They often eat small animals which are washed downstream. In very fast streams most animals live under stones or in the gravel. Ponds can also be difficult places to live in. Some ponds dry out in summer. Many animals die if the ponds dry out. Some animals produce tough eggs which lie in the dry mud until the pond fills with water again. Then the eggs hatch. Other animals move to a pond nearby if the pond they live in dries up.

Some animals only use ponds for breeding. Many frogs, insects and newts leave the water when they grow into adults.

Freshwater fish

Almost 8000 types of fish live in fresh water. This is almost as many types as live in the oceans. Most freshwater fish are bony fish but a few jawless fish and sharks live in fresh water.

There are many more types of fresh water than sea water. There are fast, mountain streams and slow, winding rivers. There are deep, cold lakes and warm, shallow ponds. Each kind of fresh water has its own special fish. Each type of fish has to cope with different problems. The hillstream fish live in mountain streams in Asia. They cling on to rocks with strong suckers. Siamese fighting fish live in ditches and have to breathe air from the surface. Killifish live in pools that dry out every summer. The adults live only for a few months. Their eggs are like seeds. They lie in the mud waiting for the pools to fill with water again.

Freshwater fish

All shapes and sizes

The shape of a fish tells us where it lives. Paddlefish and sturgeon have long 'noses'. They use these to find prey in muddy river beds. They have flat bodies and whiskers. Catfish also live on river beds. They use their whiskers, or **barbels**, to feel for food in the mud.

Hatchet fish have upturned mouths. They feed at the surface of the water. The long, thin bodies of gar and pike help them to swim among weed beds. The gar's long mouth is used to grab fish. Pike have lots of small, sharp teeth. These help them to catch other slippery fish.

Staying alive

Some fish have clever defences. The sticklebacks and perch have sharp spines along their backs. Most enemies do not like a spiky meal, so they avoid them. The electric eel and knifefish both produce electricity, which shocks their enemies. Many small fish protect themselves by swimming together in shoals. Lots of pairs of eyes help to see other fish swimming up on them.

▼ Freshwater fish come in all shapes and sizes. The largest freshwater fish is a type of sturgeon, which can grow to over six metres in length.

Water animals in danger

People have eaten water animals for thousands of years. We have caught fish ever since we first made tools. As people found better ways of catching fish, more fish were caught. Ships with strong nets were used to catch more fish. Fishermen now use special equipment to find shoals of fish in the sea. Many thousands of tons of fish and whales are caught each year. Some ships even catch fish in their breeding grounds. Many types of fish have almost died out because of these fishing methods.

Spoiling the waters

Many water animals are also killed because the waters they live in become poisoned. People have always dumped their waste in rivers and lakes. Some large towns still pump their waste, or **sewage**, into the rivers or the sea. As the numbers of people grow, so does the amount of sewage. Sewage uses up all the oxygen in the water, so the animals and plants die. Spoiling the waters like this is called **pollution**.

The oceans and seas contain huge amounts of water but some of them are becoming polluted too. Parts of the Mediterranean Sea, for example, now contain no living things at all.

Chemical waste

A more dangerous type of waste comes from factories and farms. Some factories dump their waste in rivers. Some of the waste contains **chemicals** which poison plants and animals.

▼ A dead rainbow trout floats upside down in a river. The river water has been polluted by chemical waste.

Water animals in danger

▶ Oil kills many types of water life. Oil spills out of ships when they sink at sea. A very wide area can be affected if an oil tanker is holed. Some of the oil may wash ashore, killing thousands of seashore animals.

▼ A mass of algae which has grown as a result of pouring chemicals into a river. The algae have forced the water animals to look for new homes.

Many farmers use chemicals on their land. Some chemicals are used to kill pests. Other chemicals, called **fertilizers**, help crops to grow. Many of these chemicals are washed into rivers by rain. These pest killers may kill fish or other animals in the rivers. The fertilizers make plants called **algae** grow. These plants use up all the oxygen in the water, so all the plants and animals die.

Protecting the animals

Water pollution kills plants and animals. It is also a problem for people. We need to drink water. Most water comes from rivers and lakes. Chemicals in the water affect us too. Many countries have stopped their factories from pouring chemicals into rivers. Farmers are no longer allowed to use chemicals which poison rivers. Some countries have found new ways of **treating** sewage.

There are new laws that protect some fish in the places where they breed. In some countries, fishermen may only catch a certain number of fish each year. In other countries, fishermen can only use nets which let the smaller fish escape.

All these new laws are helping to save life in the water. Hopefully, in time, all the seas and rivers will be clean and full of water animals again.

ON THE WING
Keith Porter

Introduction

▼ Birds can live in almost every habitat on Earth. This brown skua is one of the many types of bird which spend the summer in the Antarctic. The skua escapes from the very cold Antarctic winter by flying thousands of kilometres to warmer lands.

It is easy to tell birds from the other animals. Birds are the only group of animals to have **feathers**. All birds have two wings, instead of arms, and two legs. Most birds are good fliers. A few types have lost the use of their wings. These types are either fast runners or strong swimmers. The swimmers use their 'wings' as flippers.

Every bird has a bony **skeleton** with a **backbone**. Animals with backbones are called **vertebrates**. The other types of vertebrate are the **amphibians**, the **reptiles** and the **mammals**.

Birds are a very successful group of animals. They live everywhere in the world, from the hostile deserts to the busiest cities.

Birds across the world

One reason for the birds' success is their ability to fly. Birds can travel long distances over the oceans and the land. This allows them to move to warmer countries when the winter comes. Birds can also fly to safe places which other animals cannot reach, like islands in the middle of the oceans.

Introduction

The greatest numbers of birds live in the **tropical forests** where there is plenty of food. Other forest areas, the grasslands, the mountains and the deserts are all home to different types of bird. Even the cold, **polar regions** are home to many birds.

Some types of bird, like the penguin, live in only one place, or **habitat**. Others, such as the crows, live in many habitats.

▼ Many types of bird have adjusted to life in one habitat. Parrots live only in the warm tropical regions, where their food is always available.

Warm bodies

All animals need warmth to stay alive. Most animals depend on the sun to keep them warm. Birds and mammals are different. They can make heat inside their bodies, which means that they are **warm-blooded** animals.

Birds are also kept warm by their feathers. Next to their skin they have soft, short feathers called **down**. The down feathers keep the heat in and the cold out. They can be fluffed up if the weather is really cold.

The first birds

The first birds appeared about 150 million years ago, long before the first people. The world was a very different place then. It was full of plants and animals not found today. The skies were ruled by flying reptiles called the **pterosaurs** (*terror-sores*).

The first birds came from a group of early reptiles which died out many millions of years ago. This ancient group of reptiles also gave rise to the **dinosaurs** and the crocodiles. The dinosaurs died out 65 million years ago. The crocodiles are the nearest living relatives of the birds, although they look very different. Birds can be thought of as being reptiles with feathers.

▲ Archaeopteryx lived about 150 million years ago. The fossils of Archaeopteryx are important because they have shown scientists that birds came from reptiles.

▼ One of the earliest birds was Hesperornis. This bird could not fly but it was a good swimmer.

The first birds

Clues to the past

How do we know about animals of the past? When animals die, sometimes their bodies sink into the mud. Over the years, their bodies are covered by layers of mud. Over millions of years, this mud is pressed into rock. The bones and teeth of the animals become part of the rock. These remains are called **fossils**.

Scientists can tell the age of the fossils from the rocks in which the fossils are found. The scientists may be able to build a skeleton of the animal. This tells them how big the animal was, and if it walked, swam or flew. The fossils of birds are very rare. Their small bodies were often eaten by other animals.

Towards true flight

The fossil of an early bird-like animal was found in a quarry in Germany in 1861. This animal was named Archaeopteryx (*ark-e-op-terr-ix*). The skeleton looked like that of a small lizard. It had teeth, a long bony tail and wings with claws. The wings showed clear signs of having had feathers. This made Archaeopteryx very different from other reptiles of that time because they did not have feathers.

Scientists think that the **ancestors** of Archaeopteryx were tree-lizards, which leapt from tree to tree. Their clawed 'arms' helped them to grip on to the tree trunks. These reptiles gradually learned to **glide**.

Archaeopteryx probably did not fly but glided from tree to tree. It did not have a strong **breastbone** like birds do today. The breastbone is where the flight muscles are fixed.

The first true flying birds developed about 90 million years ago. They included a small seabird called Ichthyornis (*ik-thee-or-nis*).

▼ Ichthyornis is also known as 'the fish bird'. It was a seabird and led a life similar to the gulls and terns of today. Ichthyornis measured about 20 cm in length.

Thousands of types

bee hummingbird

flamingo

There are nearly 9000 types of bird in the world today. Each type of bird has its own colour pattern, or **plumage**. Each type of bird also has its own special food. This means that lots of types can live side by side. Different types do not have to fight over the same food.

The largest birds are those which have lost the use of their wings. The ostrich can be almost 2.5 m tall. The smallest birds are the hummingbirds. The Cuban bee hummingbird is only 5 cm long and weighs about 2.5 g.

As well as being very different in appearance, these birds all eat different foods. The largest bird, the ostrich, eats fruits, seeds and leaves. The eagle is an expert hunter and feeds on small land animals. The flamingo feeds on tiny animals which it finds in shallow water. The kingfisher dives into rivers and lakes when it sees fish. The woodpecker has a strong beak for digging insects out of trees. The tiny hummingbird feeds on the nectar from flowers.

bald eagle

blond-crested woodpecker

kingfisher

Thousands of types

Birds in groups

Birds are divided into groups, like all animals. These groups show us how the birds are related to one another. The 9000 types of bird are split into 28 groups, called **orders**. Each order contains birds which are alike in shape or the way in which they live. One order, for example, contains all the **birds of prey**. These include the eagles, the hawks, the falcons and the vultures. Other orders, such as the **perching birds**, contain thousands of different types. Some orders contain only one type of bird. The emu is in an order by itself.

▶ All birds belong to one of 28 orders. Each order is divided into families. Each family is divided into individual types, or species.

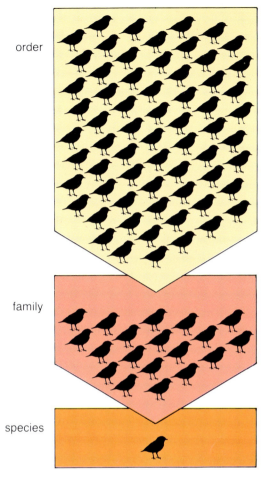

ostrich

A family likeness

Almost all of the orders are split into **families**. Some families include birds which look alike. For example, the four members of the flamingo family are exactly the same shape. They differ only in size and colour. Flamingos are all different shades of pink. The penguins, the turkeys, the kingfishers and many other bird families also share a family likeness.

Most families include birds which have the same **habits**. This may mean that they live in the same place, like the woodpecker family which lives in the forests, or the gull family which lives near the sea. It may also mean that they eat the same type of food. For example, all the hummingbird family drinks **nectar** from flowers.

A bird's body

The bodies of birds are light and strong. Their skeletons have many hollow bones which reduce their weight. These bones are kept strong by tiny supports inside the bones.

Like many animals, birds have **lungs** for breathing. Unlike other animals, the birds also have balloons of air in their bodies called **air-sacs**. The air-sacs hold the air as it is breathed in. The air then passes to the lungs in a continual flow. This way, air moves through the lungs all the time, giving the birds as much **oxygen** as possible.

Bird senses

All birds have good eyesight in order to see ahead when they are flying. Most birds use their eyes for hunting. The birds of prey have the best eyesight of all.

Many birds have very good hearing. Birds often use 'songs' to talk to one another. Few birds have a good sense of smell or taste. Most birds find their food by its colour or shape.

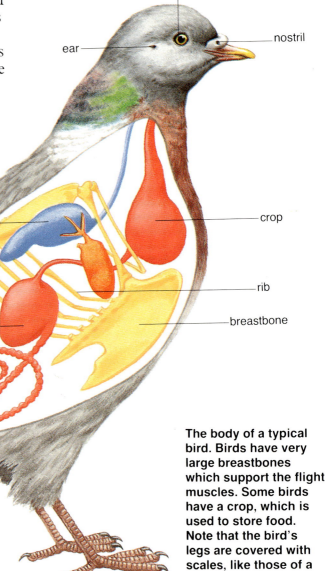

The body of a typical bird. Birds have very large breastbones which support the flight muscles. Some birds have a crop, which is used to store food. Note that the bird's legs are covered with scales, like those of a lizard.

A bird's body

Beaks

A bird's beak is a very important tool. Birds use their beaks to pick things up. Most birds use their beaks to build their nests. Beaks can carry mud, sticks or grass.

Most of the beak is made of bone. Around the bone there is a layer of horny material. This is called **keratin**. A bird's feathers and our fingernails are also made of keratin.

Beaks come in all shapes and sizes. Different shapes are needed to feed on different foods. Long, thin beaks are used to probe into mud for worms. Strong, hooked beaks are used for tearing up food. The sharp beaks of the woodpeckers are used to bore into trees.

Feathers

Feathers are very important to birds. Feathers keep the heat in and the cold and water out. They also help birds to fly and provide **camouflage** on the ground. Each bird has several shapes of feather. The broad, long feathers make up the wings. The shorter, fine feathers cover the outside of the body.

The feathers are replaced at least once a year. As the old ones drop out, or **moult**, the new ones grow. Birds spend a lot of time cleaning and oiling their feathers. This is called **preening** and is done by using the beak as a comb.

▲ The beaks of these birds are shaped to eat different foods. The beak of the eagle tears up meat. The beak of the chaffinch crushes hard seeds. The pelican has a pouch for catching fish. The beak of the oystercatcher opens shells.

◀ The wing of a bird has feathers of several shapes. The feathers combine to form a strong, light wing which keeps the bird in the air with the minimum of effort.

How birds fly

People have always wished that they could fly like birds. We do not have wings and our bodies are too heavy. If we jump into the air, our strength gives us the **lift** to get us off the ground. It is our weight which brings us down again. Birds are light animals and they have strong flight muscles which flap their wings. The lift that the wings produce overcomes their weight so the birds can fly.

Wings and wind

The shape of a bird's wing is very important. As it cuts through the air, the wing's shape helps to give the bird lift. The air passing over the top of the wing has further to go than the air passing beneath the wing. The result is that the air beneath pushes the wing upwards.

▲ The wing movements of a bird in flight.

The flapping of a bird's wing pushes it through the air in the same way that swimmers push their way through the water. The wings give the bird forward movement, or **thrust**. During flight, the bird's wings twist and turn. Attached to the breastbone are a large pair of muscles which pull the wings down against the air. A smaller pair of muscles pull the wings back over the body.

◀ A mute swan taking off. Swans need to build up speed before they can lift themselves into the air.

How birds fly

When you ride a bicycle, you feel the wind in your hair. This is the pull, or the **drag**, of the air. If you crouch down into a smooth shape you will go faster. Look at a bird's shape in the air. It is smooth and **streamlined**. The bird's shape helps it to overcome the drag.

Riding on air

Air rises when it is warm. Once a bird is in the air, it can make use of the rising air currents, called **thermals**. If the thermals are strong enough, they will lift a bird up high without it having to flap its wings.

Some large birds, such as eagles and vultures, have wings which are shaped to gain as much advantage as possible from the rising air. These birds are called **soaring birds**.

When a soaring bird has reached a great height, it can glide a long way without any effort. As it glides, it searches for another thermal to take it up high again.

▼ An albatross is a large, soaring bird. The long, thin wings are shaped to get as much lift as possible from the strong sea breezes. The albatross finds it much more difficult to fly on a calm day when there is no wind to provide lift.

Dance and courtship

Much of a bird's life is spent bringing up its young. Most birds produce young, or **breed**, at least once every year. Some birds raise many **broods** of young in their lifetimes. In order to produce young, a male and a female need to form a **pair**.

The first step towards the forming of a pair is when the male bird chooses a place to nest. Once a good place is found, the male sets up his **territory**. The territory is the area in which he will bring up his family. The male tells other birds where his territory is by singing.

A fierce display

The male birds often have to put on fierce dances, or **displays**, to keep control of their territory. Many warn off **intruders** with their loud songs. The strongest, most colourful and noisiest males get the best territory.

Birds usually avoid actual fighting. Each male soon learns where his neighbour's territory ends. Most types of bird have bushes, trees, or posts which they use as territory markers, or signing points.

Different types of bird need different sizes of territory. A large eagle needs many square kilometres to gather food for its young. A tiny wren needs only 50 square metres. The size of the territory depends upon how much food can be found, and how much each bird needs.

▲ A selection of different courtship acts. The hawfinches rub beaks. The European robins offer each other food. The penguin performs a dance. The bird of paradise displays his plumage.

Dance and courtship

Courtship

If a female bird comes into the male's territory, the male will dance or display in front of her. This is called **courtship**. The male attracts the female in a variety of ways. Some males simply move their wings or their head. Other birds, like peacocks, use their colourful feathers to make a beautiful display. Some of the finest displays are made by the birds of paradise. Each male bird has a different shape and colour pattern. They use their colourful crests, frills or long tails to attract the females.

The male frigate bird and the umbrella bird have unusual displays. They blow out red pouches which are on their necks. The females are attracted to the males with the biggest and brightest pouches.

Some pairs, like the grebes, dance together. Other birds offer each other pieces of food. These acts make sure that the pair stays together. Most pairs will stay together for one year. Some pairs will stay together for life.

▼ A male frigate bird displays its bright red pouch to a female.

Nests and eggs

Nests are the places where birds bring up their families. The nests are built to protect the eggs and the young birds. Many animals like to eat eggs or young birds. To prevent this, most nests are built in places which are difficult for other animals to reach. Cliffs, trees and burrows are all safe places for nests.

▼ The nest of a weaver bird hangs from a branch. This type of weaver bird builds its nest close to the nests of other weaver birds.

▲ The simple nest of a mallard duck hidden among some reeds. The nest is lined with soft feathers.

All shapes and sizes

Every type of bird has a different sort of nest. All nests must be big enough for the parent bird to sit on.

The simplest nests are platforms made of twigs or leaves. The insides of the nests are often lined with moss or feathers. More complex nests have 'roofs' added. This makes a hollow, ball-like nest. The eggs are kept warm and dry inside.

The most complex nests are built by the weaver birds. These birds **weave** grass into a strong ball-shaped basket. Swallows and ovenbirds build their nests out of mud. The mud then sets into a hard clay.

Some nests are well protected. The nests of the broadbills and the sunbirds are hung from branches. Other birds make tiny entrances to their nests, so **predators** cannot reach the young. The female hornbill seals herself inside a hollow tree until her eggs hatch. The male passes food to her through a tiny hole.

Nests and eggs

Birds' eggs

A bird's egg is a tiny, enclosed world. The hard shell protects the growing bird inside. The shell is made from a kind of chalk. The egg white, or **albumen**, is a fluid which protects the **yolk**. The yolk is full of food. On the surface of the yolk is a tiny spot. This is the beginning of the new bird. The egg must be kept warm while the tiny bird grows inside. The parents have to sit on the egg to keep it warm. This is called **incubation**.

Some birds lay up to 20 eggs in one nest. All the eggs in a nest are about the same size. The eggs which are laid on the ground are coloured to match their surroundings, such as stones, gravel or sand. The eggs which are laid in hidden nests can be white, yellow or blue.

The birds which nest on cliffs, such as the guillemots have pointed eggs. These eggs are shaped to roll around in a circle. This stops them from rolling over the edge of the cliff.

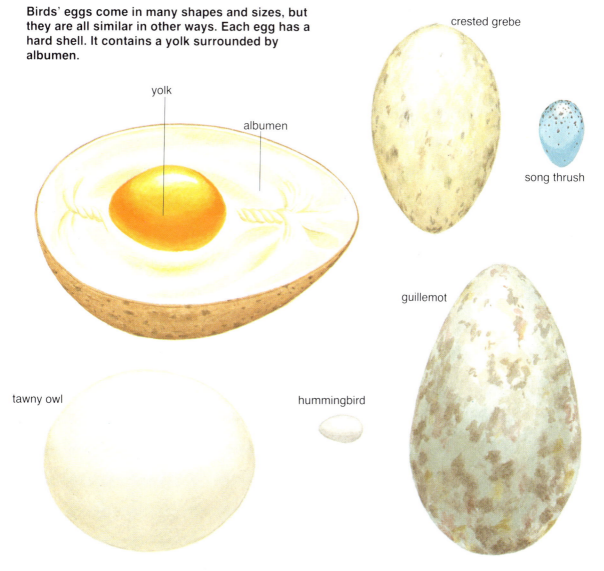

Birds' eggs come in many shapes and sizes, but they are all similar in other ways. Each egg has a hard shell. It contains a yolk surrounded by albumen.

The young bird

When a young bird is ready to hatch, it has to force its way into the world. Just before hatching, the young bird grows a hard bump on its beak. This bump is called an egg tooth. The tiny bird uses the egg tooth to break through the eggshell.

Care of the young

Young birds can be divided into two main types, **chicks** and **nestlings**. The chicks have fluffy bodies and can move about as soon as they hatch. The chicks stay close to their mother, following her wherever she goes. The mother leads the chicks to food. Most chicks are patterned, or camouflaged. If the chicks are alarmed, they stay still to match their surroundings. This helps to protect them from their enemies.

▲ A blue tit feeding its nestlings. Their wide, gaping mouths demand food from their parents. The young blue tits stay in the nest for up to 21 days.

◀ An albatross lays a single egg which it incubates for two months. After hatching, the young bird is fed by the parents for a further nine months. The nestling has long down feathers to keep it warm.

The young bird

The nestlings have to stay in the nest after hatching. All the nestlings are blind, naked and helpless when they hatch. They have to be fed by their parents. This is a non-stop job for the parent birds. Some of the smaller types of bird have to make up to 900 trips each day hunting for insects. The birds of prey and seabirds only feed their young once or twice a day. They hunt for larger meals such as rabbits or fish.

The nestlings of small birds, such as the tits or the chickadees, stay in the nest for about 20 days. The nestlings of larger birds stay in the nest for much longer. The albatross nestling does not leave the nest until it is nine months old.

Leaving the nest

After the nestlings leave the nest, they are called **fledgelings**. The fledgelings from one nest usually stay together. They still depend on their parents for food and protection. The cries of the young birds guide the parents to them at feeding time.

Some fledgelings leave the nest before they can fly. This is a time of great danger. Many fledgelings are eaten by predators. Some parent birds put themselves in danger by trying to lead an attacker away from their young. Other parent birds will strike out at an attacker.

The young bird is safer when it has learnt to fly. Some young birds, like the swift, can fly on long journeys as soon as they leave the nest. Larger birds, like the Californian condor, can take many months before they develop their flying skills.

▼ An adult booby spreads its wings as an angry warning. The eggs would soon be taken if they were left unguarded.

The long journeys

Many types of bird breed in the far northern and southern parts of the world. The winters in these places are cold and harsh. The insects, fruit and other foods disappear. As the winter approaches, the birds fly on long journeys to warmer countries. The birds will return when the spring comes. This type of journey is called a **migration**. Some birds fly very long distances when they migrate. The Arctic terns, for example, fly all the way from the Arctic to the Antarctic.

Some birds from hot countries leave their homes as the summer approaches. These **migrants** leave because all their food dries up in the hot, dry season.

Which birds migrate?

There are three main types of migrant. These are the summer visitors, the winter visitors and the birds of passage.

The best known summer visitors are the common, or barn, swallows. They breed all over northern America, Europe, and Asia. In the autumn, the American swallows fly to South America. At the same time, the European swallows fly to central Africa. Other summer visitors to the northern countries include the sand martins and the red-eyed vireos.

The winter visitors are the birds which breed in the Arctic. They include many types of goose, duck and wading bird. The snow geese and the blue geese breed in the Canadian Arctic. In the autumn, they fly south to the United States. The brent geese, the greylags and the whooper swans make a similar journey in Europe. They move south to feed along the warmer coasts.

Birds of passage are birds which are on the move. They can travel from the far north to the deep south. Each year the sanderlings and the American golden plovers pass over the United States. The common crane is a typical European bird of passage. It breeds in Scandinavia and winters in Africa.

▼ Cranes migrating south. Migrating birds often fly in a V-shaped formation. The leading birds create a 'wake' of air which has a sucking effect. This allows the birds behind to fly with less effort.

The long journeys

Finding the way

Some birds travel thousands of kilometres during their migrations. These birds always return to the same nest the next season. Scientists have tried to find out how the birds find their way. Many ideas have been suggested, but none give a full answer to the puzzle. Some birds follow the rivers or the coasts. Perhaps they learn the way? Many birds migrate at night. They cannot see the rivers or the land. **Experiments** have shown us that some birds find their way by using the stars.

◀ A group of house martins gather before their long flight from northern Europe to Africa.

▼ The Arctic tern breeds in the far north of America and Europe. The birds fly to the southern tips of America and Africa when the winter comes. Some Arctic terns journey even further, reaching Antarctica.

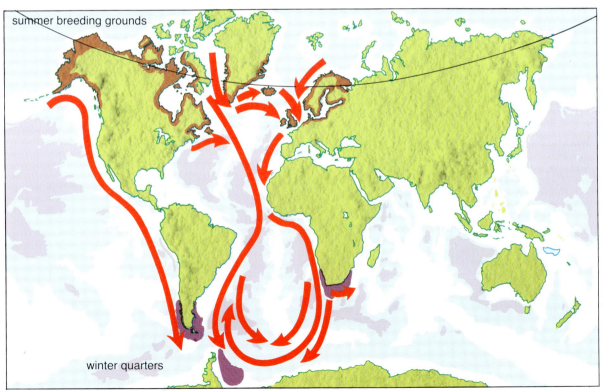

The polar regions

Why do so many migrant birds breed in the Arctic and the Antarctic? Their long journeys are exhausting. Why do they not live in the warmer countries? The answer is that the cold polar regions are rich in food. During the short spring and summer, lots of plants and insects appear. The seas are full of tiny sea animals and fish.

Most birds of the polar regions have to leave as the winter approaches. The land and the sea freeze over.

Antarctic birds

Most of Antarctica is an icy desert. Nothing can live or grow on the snow and ice. Only the coasts offer food and shelter. The Antarctic birds all depend on the sea for food.

During the summer, the ice breaks up over the sea. The gulls and the petrels make their nests along the coasts. When the ice returns, they have to move north in search of the open sea.

Penguins are well known Antarctic birds. The 16 types of penguin all live along the cold southern shores. Their bodies are used to the cold. Under their skin is a thick layer of fat. The fat helps to keep out the bitter cold. Penguins have lost the use of their wings. Their wings are used like flippers for swimming. Some penguins can swim at 60 kph underwater.

▼ A Dominican gull perches on an iceberg in Antarctica. The gull is a threat to other birds because it steals their eggs.

The polar regions

The Emperor penguins are the only birds which can stay inland during the winter. The winter is when they breed. The male stands over the single egg, keeping it warm beneath his body. He does not move for weeks.

Arctic birds

The northern lands of Canada, Greenland and Scandinavia are all parts of the Arctic. Many birds live in the Arctic during the summer. In the winter, the land is bleak and frozen. In the summer, the boggy land provides plenty of food.

Most birds arrive in the Arctic just as the snow melts. The birds have to breed before the ice returns. Many types of geese, duck and wading bird nest in the Arctic.

The seas of the Arctic are rich in food. Many types of gull, skua and tern breed along the Arctic coasts. Birds called auks swim in the sea in search of food.

A few birds, like the willow grouse and the ptarmigan, stay on the edges of the Arctic all through the winter.

▲ Emperor penguins are the largest of the penguins. They stand one metre tall and weigh about 30 kg.

▼ The snowy owl is an Arctic predator. It stays in the Arctic throughout the year. The snowy owl feeds on small mammals and birds.

Seabirds

The seas and oceans, which cover much of the Earth, are rich in food. Birds which get their food from the sea are called seabirds. Most seabirds live along the coasts or on islands. A few seabirds can be found far from the land.

There are about 250 types of seabird. The tropicbirds, skimmers, boobies and frigate birds live in the warm tropical seas. The guillemots and razorbills live in the cold northern seas. The penguins and sheathbills are examples from the cold southern seas. Some types, like the gulls, petrels and terns, fly over all the seas.

How are seabirds different?

A life at sea would not suit most land birds. They could not survive in the strong winds and waves. Seabirds have strong bodies and most of them are larger than the land birds. Seabirds have wings which are shaped to help them glide on the strong sea breezes. Some are long distance travellers. Each year, they fly from the northern seas to the southern seas.

The bodies of most seabirds are kept warm and dry by **waterproof** feathers. They keep these feathers well oiled by preening. Some seabirds, like the cormorants, do not have waterproof feathers. They have to dry themselves by spreading out their wings and 'sunbathing'. Birds that live in the cold seas have a layer of fat under their skin to help keep them warm.

Most seabirds can float on the sea. They swim by using their large **webbed feet** as paddles. Some types can dive underwater in search of fish. Gannets and boobies dive like arrows from heights of 30 m. They have very strong skulls to survive the shock of hitting the water from this height. Some diving seabirds have special 'see through' eyelids which help them to see underwater.

◀ Cormorants are seabirds which dive into the sea to catch fish. They spread out their wings to dry them when they return to land.

▶ A noisy colony of gannets on the coast of New Zealand. The young birds have black and white speckled coats. They will fly 2000 km to the coast of Australia when they are fully grown. The parent birds will stay within a few hundred kilometres of the breeding site.

Seabirds

Bird colonies

All seabirds lay their eggs on land. Most seabirds breed every year. Seabirds often make their nests in large groups or **colonies**. Some colonies contain tens of thousands of birds. Gannets and guillemots often nest on the ledges of cliffs. Huge colonies of gulls and terns nest on gravel banks along the coasts. Other birds, such as the albatrosses, nest together on remote islands.

Why do some seabirds nest in colonies? One reason is that many birds will gather where there is a lot of food. Another reason is that living in a colony is safer. Many animals, including birds, will eat eggs and young birds. The adult birds, like gulls and terns, help each other to defend the colony. This makes it more difficult for the predators to eat the eggs and young birds.

◀ A group of terns has spotted a shoal of fish. Each bird waits for a fish to come near to the surface. One bird has dived to grab a fish with its beak.

Wetland birds

Streams, rivers, lakes and **marshes** are all wetland areas. The wetlands are the homes for many types of bird. These birds are found in many parts of the world, from the cold, boggy lands of the north, to the hot, steamy swamps of the tropical lands.

Some wetland birds, like the ducks and the grebes, are called swimmers. Others, such as the herons, plovers and sandpipers, are called **waders**. The waders are birds which feed in mud or shallow water.

Swimmers

Swimmers include geese, swans, ducks, grebes and the divers. Altogether there are about 175 types. Most swimming birds are adapted for a life on the water. Their feathers are waterproof, like those of the seabirds. Most swimmers also have webbed feet which they use like paddles.

Geese, swans and many types of duck eat plants. Some types of goose and swan nibble water plants. Others come ashore to **graze** like cattle. A few types, like the teal and mallard ducks, look for food in the mud. Other types of duck use their bills to **filter** tiny plants and animals from the water.

Some types of duck, grebe and diver eat small fish, frogs and insects. The black-throated diver, or Arctic loon, searches for its food underwater. Its smooth shape and large feet make it a good underwater swimmer. The canvasback and the tufted duck feed on plants and animals. They dive down to feed on the beds of rivers and lakes.

Waders and others

There are over 400 types of wading bird. Some have long legs and necks. Others have thin beaks which probe into the mud for food. These birds, like the snipes and curlews, usually spend the winter along the coasts. In the summer, they breed on the wet moorlands and marshes. They feed on small animals buried in the mud or soil. Storks, herons and cranes are other waders. They have long legs and strong, sharp beaks. They use their beaks to spear fish and frogs. These birds hunt in shallow lakes and rivers.

▼ Some of the ways in which wetland birds feed. Some wade near the shore in search of food. The surface swimmers feed on underwater plants and animals. Others swim deep below the surface. The non-swimmers grab prey which comes close to the surface.

Wetland birds

▶ A pair of mallard ducks. The male is the brightly coloured one. Mallard ducks feed on small animals, plants and seeds.

▲ Flamingos are wading birds. They have a special way of feeding. A flamingo's tongue forces water through the bill. The bill catches the food particles and tiny animals which float in water.

ducks

There are some 130 types of wetland bird which are neither swimmers nor waders. Dippers are small birds which live alongside fast flowing mountain streams. They walk underwater along the beds of streams in search of water insects and small fish. The colourful kingfishers hunt from perches above rivers and streams. These birds catch fish by diving swiftly into the water.

Birds in the open

Parts of the world are covered with large, grassy areas with few trees. These areas are called the grasslands. They include the **prairies** of North America and the **savannas** of Africa.

The open grasslands can be difficult places for birds to live. Most grasslands are dry and windy. It may not rain for months. Many grassland birds have to fly long distances in search of food and water. Trees are safe places for birds to build their nests, but there are few trees in the grasslands. They have to make nests on the ground, where predators can find them more easily. Animals such as coyotes, foxes and snakes like to eat the young birds.

Nests on the ground

Many grassland birds have learnt how to hide their eggs. Some, like the larks, build their nests inside clumps of grass. Others, like the grouse and prairie chickens, lay their eggs on the ground. Their nests are just small hollows, or **scrapes**, in the ground. The nests in the open contain dull, speckled eggs which are difficult to see. The eggs are well protected when the mother is on the nest. Her camouflaged plumage hides the eggs.

A few grassland birds build their nests in burrows. The American burrowing owl uses the burrows of prairie dogs. Some ovenbirds use the burrows of mice or gophers. The red ovenbird builds a round, mud nest which is like a small fort.

▼ A well camouflaged willow grouse sits quietly on her nest. The willow grouse grows white feathers in winter, to blend in with the snow.

Birds in the open

▲ A burrowing owl stands near to its nest in a prairie dog's tunnel. It keeps a sharp lookout for its prey, such as mice or lizards.

▼A comparison, to scale, of the rhea, emu and ostrich. They are all grassland birds. Although these birds look alike, they do not belong to the same family.

Large running birds

The largest birds in the world live in the grasslands. These include the ostrich, the emu and the rhea. The ostrich lives only in Africa. It grows to 2.5 m in height and can run at 60 kph. The emu lives only in Australia. The two types of rhea live only in South America. Rheas are now rare birds. Many have been killed for food and because they eat the farmers' crops.

All these birds have lost the use of their wings over millions of years. They no longer need to fly from their enemies. Instead, they have long, strong legs for running. Their speed, size, good eyesight and sharp beaks help to protect them.

The nests of ostriches, emus and rheas are all simple scrapes in the ground. Male ostriches and rheas often look after the young. They form 'herds' of the young from several nests. The emus usually nest alone.

Birds in deserts

Deserts are very dry places. During the day, they can be very hot, but at night they can be bitterly cold. These changes from hot to cold, and the lack of water make the deserts very difficult places to live in. Even so, some types of bird only live in deserts. Most desert birds are light in colour, which helps to camouflage them.

Desert birds need to keep cool. The roadrunners and the coursers have long legs to help them. Their long legs keep their bodies off the very hot ground. The air is much cooler just above the surface. Most desert birds cannot stand the great heat and have to rest in the shade in the middle of the day.

▲ Water holes can be dangerous places. Predators wait nearby, so drinking is done as quickly as possible. Some of the flock keeps watch while the other birds drink.

▼ A male sandgrouse collecting water for his family. The water is carried in his belly feathers.

Birds in deserts

◀ Mourning doves are well suited to a life in hot, dry regions. They can survive without water much longer than most birds. This mourning dove has made its nest in a cactus tree.

The need for water

All plants and animals need water to stay alive. Some desert animals have bodies which can go without water for many days. Most desert birds need water every day. Seed eaters need water often because their food is so dry. They have to live close enough to fly to the water holes. Desert birds have one advantage over the other desert animals. The birds can fly a long way to reach water. The sandgrouse can fly up to 90 km each day to water holes.

There are 16 types of sandgrouse. Some drink only at night. Others travel to the water holes in the mornings or the evenings. The male sandgrouse have a clever way of bringing water to their young. They use their belly feathers like a bath sponge. After drinking, the male sits in the water to fill his 'sponge'. Then he flies back to the nest. The chicks drink the water which has been soaked up by his belly feathers.

Some small birds, like finches, get enough water from the plants which they eat. They do not have to fly to get water from far away.

Feeding and breeding

Birds need plenty of food and water when they are nesting. Most desert birds feed on plants or insects. In the desert, the plants and insects are only plentiful when there has been rain. These birds must breed when the rains come. Only then can they gather enough food and water for themselves and their young. Some birds can only nest once every few years. Other desert birds, like the roadrunner, eat lizards and snakes. These birds do not have to wait for the rain before they gather enough food to breed.

Mourning doves feed their young with 'pigeon milk'. This is a very rich food which is mixed in the throat, or **crop**, of the adult birds. The dove chicks grow very quickly on this food.

The eggs and the young need to be protected from the hot sun. Small birds, such as the desert wheatears, nest in burrows or crevices to escape from the sun. Other birds, such as the coursers and pratincoles, stand over their eggs to shade them. The Egyptian plovers cool their eggs and chicks with water.

Birds in rain forests

Forests in the hot, steamy parts of the Earth, close to the **Equator**, are called tropical rain forests. These forests contain over half of all the types of bird in the world.

The rain forests can be divided into three main layers. Each layer of a rain forest contains many places for animals to live. The forest floor is dark, damp and warm. It is thick with bushes and tree trunks. The middle layer includes climbing creepers and small trees. Above this, giant trees form a roof of branches, or a **canopy**, over the forest.

The forest floor

The birds which live on the forest floor usually have strong, pointed beaks and short, broad wings. Many forest floor birds hop or run along the ground. It is difficult to fly among all the tree trunks. Some birds find their food on the forest floor. The colourful pittas, for example, hunt for insects, snails and spiders.

Some birds, like the cotingas, lyrebirds and peacocks fly down to small clearings in the forest floor for **courtship dances**. These dances attract the females. Some cotingas, such the male cock-of-the-rock, are very brightly coloured.

The male bowerbirds build 'tunnels' of sticks to attract the females. The males decorate their tunnels with coloured feathers, stones and flowers.

▶ A male cock-of-the-rock perching close to his display ground. If a female comes near, the male will fly down to the forest floor and try to attract her by performing a dance.

Birds in rain forests

▲ Rainbow lorikeets wander through Australian forests in search of food. They feed on the nectar from flowers and on insects. Lorikeets belong to the parrot family.

▲ The length of the toucan's beak gives the bird a long reach. The beak is used also for display.

Above the ground

The middle layer of the forest, between the ground and the treetops, is full of birds. The birds feed on the many insects, fruits and leaves. Large flocks of birds wander in search of food. Each flock may contain a mixture of birds. They feel safer in large numbers. The fruit and seed eaters include the barbets, birds of paradise and the parrots. The insect eaters include the motmots, broadbills and the manakins.

One of the finest groups are the American hummingbirds. They feed mainly on the nectar from flowers. They also eat a few insects. The sunbirds of Asia and Africa feed in the same way.

Above the trees

The birds which live in the forest canopy include the tanagers, the toucans, the hornbills and the cotingas. The hornbills and the toucans have long colourful beaks. They use their beaks to reach the fruit on the thinnest of branches. Many of these birds spend their whole lives in the canopy.

Birds of prey also live in the canopy. The harpy eagle and the Philippine monkey eagle eat monkeys and other small animals.

Birds in woodlands

▼ Members of the finch family are found in many parts of the world. The hawfinch is a very shy bird, often living unseen in the trees. Its strong beak can break open the hardest seeds. The hawfinch lives in European woodlands.

Many parts of the world contain forests called woodlands. These forests have four **seasons**, the spring, the summer, the autumn and the winter. The woodlands are green, warm places in the spring and summer. There are lots of insects, buds and seeds for the birds to eat. In spring, the woodlands echo with the songs of the birds. This is the time when the male birds set up their territories. Each male sings to warn off any intruders. The woodland trees lose their leaves each autumn. By the winter, the woodlands are bare and cold. Food for the birds becomes scarce.

Finding food

Some woodland birds avoid the winter by migrating. These include the flycatchers and the warblers, which eat only insects. The migrant birds leave the woodlands in the autumn and fly to the warmer countries in search of insects.

Other woodland birds stop eating insects in the autumn. They feed on nuts, fruit and seeds during the winter. The larger woodland birds are often predators. The predators survive all the year around by feeding on other birds and small mammals, such as mice.

Birds in woodlands

Three kinds of woodland birds

bullfinch

magpie

flycatcher

Insect eaters and others

Many woodland birds eat insects. The treecreepers use their sharp beaks to pick the insects from the tree **bark**. The flycatchers, the vireos and the warblers eat the insects from the leaves of bushes and trees.

The woodpeckers are among the largest insect eaters. They have sharp beaks which cut into trees in search of insect **grubs**. Woodpeckers have very strong heads, which take the shock of the hammering. They also have very long tongues with sticky tips. Some types of woodpecker use their sticky tongues to catch ants deep in their nests.

Some woodpeckers and other types of bird store nuts for the winter. The American acorn woodpecker stores acorns in tree trunks. Several birds may use one tree. They guard the tree from other birds. Magpies, jays and crows also store nuts and acorns. Other birds hide insects and small animals. Birds make these stores in the summer when food is plentiful.

Bud and seed eaters

Birds of the finch family eat buds and seeds. Each type of finch has a different shaped beak. The hawfinches have short, stout beaks. They can crack open hard seeds, such as cherry stones. The goldfinches have beaks like tweezers. They pick the seeds from flowers. The chaffinches have small pointed beaks and eat small seeds. The bullfinches have short, rounded beaks and eat leaf buds.

▶ Acorn woodpeckers live in groups. They work together to gather acorns and care for the young.

The northern forests

The northern forests stretch across the far north of America, Europe and Asia. These forests are called the **coniferous forests**. The trees, which include pines, firs and spruces, keep their needle-like leaves all through the year.

The winters in the northern forests are very long and cold. The forest birds can only breed in the short summers. Many of the birds are only summer visitors. They fly to the forests to breed. They return south to the warmer lands in the autumn. A small number of birds manage to live in the northern forests all the year around.

Surviving the winter

The northern forests provide the birds with little food during the harsh winter. Much of the ground is frozen solid and covered with snow. The birds have to survive in temperatures as low as minus 35°C. Most birds of the northern forests, such as the nutcrackers, eat seeds, nuts and leaves. Some, like the crossbills, prefer one kind of food. Each type of crossbill only eats the seeds from one kind of tree.

Some birds move to the forests for shelter in the winter. Grouse and capercaillies move from the open, snow-covered plains to the forests. They survive by eating the leaves of the conifers. Few other birds are able to eat these leaves.

The birds must keep warm or they will die of cold in the winter. The feathers of the northern birds are often very fluffy. The grouse have more feathers than other birds. The extra feathers help to keep the warmth in and the cold out.

Owls and hawks

The northern forests are home to many small mammals such as the voles, shrews, hares and lemmings. These animals are eaten by the birds of prey. These birds include the eagles, hawks, falcons and owls.

▲ The common crossbill feeds mainly on the seeds of spruce trees. Other crossbills eat the seeds of the larch and pine trees.

The northern forests

Birds of prey have very good eyesight. They can see the tiniest movement of any animal. The buzzards and goshawks catch small mammals and birds. The peregrine falcons and sparrowhawks catch mainly birds.

Many of the small animals come out to feed at night. They are hunted by the northern owls which include the snowy owls, the horned owls and the eagle owls. These birds are large enough to catch small deer or foxes. Owls have very good hearing as well as good eyesight. They use both these senses to hunt their prey.

In the summer, most birds of prey move further north to nest. Many other birds of prey fly into the northern forests from the warmer countries. They usually build their nests high in the trees.

▲ Peregrine falcons kill birds in mid-air by diving on them at great speed. Their prey include pigeons, ducks and grouse.

▼ A male capercaillie defends his territory by crying out an angry warning to other males which might be nearby.

Mountain birds

Mountains are bare, rocky places. The tops of many mountains are covered with snow and ice. Strong winds blow and the air is thin. Few types of bird can live on the mountains. The high winds, the cold, and a lack of food keep many birds away.

The birds that do live on mountains are either birds of prey, or small perching birds. The birds of prey are strong enough to fly in the high winds. They survive by eating other animals. The small perching birds avoid the wind. They live by clinging to the mountains.

Hunters and scavengers

The mountain birds of prey include hunters and birds which feed on dead animals, called **scavengers**. The hunters, such as the eagles, kill small animals. They kill by using their clawed feet, or **talons**. The golden eagle dives on to its prey at speeds of up to 90 kph.

The vultures and the condors are the largest scavengers. They may feed away from the mountains. Both vultures and the condors make good use of the wind. They can **soar** and glide over long distances. Some types can soar to over 7500 m. The bearded vulture, or lammergeier, is an unusual scavenger. It has learned to feed on the inner part, or **marrow**, of large bones. The bird drops the bones from the air to break them open.

◀ Eagles normally lay between two and four eggs. This is a golden eagle family. The young need plenty of food. The adult males do most of the hunting. They fly many kilometres in search of prey. The golden eagle kills animals as large as hares.

Mountain birds

▲ A lammergeier soars high up in the sky. Lammergeiers spend much of their time searching for dead animals. Lammergeiers are not killers.

▼ Long toes help the wallcreeper to cling to steep rock faces. Wallcreepers make their nests on small ledges. The young stay in the nests until they are nearly full grown.

Perching birds

The mountains have a winter and a summer like other places, or habitats. In the summer, the rocky ledges and the mountain slopes are covered with flowers. Some small birds feed on the insects and seeds found among these plants. In the winter, many of the smaller birds move further down the mountains.

The small birds survive on the mountains because they stay close to the ground. They would be blown away by the strong winds if they tried to fly very far from the ground.

The choughs and the wallcreepers have **adapted** to life on the mountains. Both types of bird search for insects on the rocky ledges and **crags**. The wallcreepers can walk up or down the steepest cliffs.

City life

Birds live wherever they can find food. Many birds live in our towns and cities where there is plenty of food. The houses, roads, shops and factories have driven most other animals away. Birds have learned to live in the most difficult surroundings. They can fly above the dangerous traffic. Many birds use the buildings to perch on, and as nesting sites.

Nesting sites

The city and town birds have two types of nesting site. Some, like the thrushes, use the green parts of the cities. They nest in the bushes and trees of the gardens and parks. Others, such as the sparrows, the pigeons and the starlings, nest in the buildings. These birds are common in the cities. They have learned to change their habits to suit their surroundings.

The birds which nest on the buildings treat them like cliffs. The window ledges of tall buildings are sometimes used by gulls and falcons. Starlings nest in the roofs of the buildings. They use the roofs in the same way as other birds use trees.

The swallows, the swifts and the martins are used to making their homes in buildings. These birds build their mud nests under the **eaves** of the roofs. The North American chimney swift lives a dangerous life. It makes its nest inside a chimney. Luckily, this bird breeds in the summer when most chimneys are not in use. The swift nests inside hollow trees in the country.

▼ Pigeons are distantly related to the rock dove which nests on cliffs. Tall buildings in cities provide similar nest sites for pigeons.

City life

Different food

The sparrows and the pigeons eat seeds and leaves in the country. The swallows and the swifts catch flying insects. The starlings eat both plants and insects. The falcons eat small animals. These birds cannot find much food like this in the cities.

The city birds have to eat different kinds of food. Many survive on the scraps of food that we throw away. Birds pick through our rubbish for food. Food is scarce for all birds during the winter. Some birds depend on people to leave out food for them.

▶ City birds flock to the squares where they search for food. Many birds know that people will feed them. These birds have little fear of people.

▼ A swallow's nest in the roof of a building. This European swallow will fly 11 000 km to southern Africa when the winter draws near.

Birds on islands

▼ Guillemots and razorbills crowd on to the rocky cliffs of an island in the Atlantic Ocean. No food is available on the island. All the birds catch fish from the sea.

Islands are areas of land surrounded by water. Some islands are very small, while other islands are hundreds of kilometres wide. All islands can be divided into two main types. The islands which are close to the land, or **mainland**, are called offshore islands. Other islands are found far out to sea. They are called oceanic islands. Most birds and other animals can reach offshore islands. The oceanic islands cannot be reached by most animals, unless they are taken there by people. Birds, however, can reach the bleakest and loneliest of islands.

Most oceanic islands are formed when **volcanoes** appear from under the sea. These islands are just bare rock to begin with. The plants and the animals arrive over a long period of time. Some are blown on to the islands, while others float to the islands. Birds are some of the first animals to arrive on these islands. Many types of animal never reach oceanic islands.

Nesting sites

Both types of island are visited by the seabirds. These birds use the islands only as nesting sites. They find their food in the sea. The offshore islands are used because most egg eating animals live on the mainland. The seabirds nest in huge colonies on these safe islands. Sometimes whole cliffs become white with their droppings. The oceanic islands are also very important to the seabirds. They may be the only nesting sites for thousands of kilometres. They are also safe places to nest as the only predators are some other types of seabird.

Birds on islands

New types of bird

Flocks of small birds are sometimes blown to oceanic islands by chance. Usually, small birds would not cross the huge oceans. The first birds to reach an oceanic island are very lucky. They do not have to share their food with others. If a small flock arrives, some may begin to eat the seeds. Others may prefer to eat the insects. The beaks of these birds will change shape over thousands of years. The birds become different types, or **species**. This has happened on many islands in the Pacific Ocean.

The islands of Hawaii once contained 22 types of honeycreeper. Some of these have died out now. Scientists believe that all the honeycreepers came from one type of bird. The Galapagos islands have 13 types of finch. All these finches arose from one type of finch.

Some birds are found only on islands. The Caribbean islands each have their own type of hummingbird. The kiwi birds of New Zealand and the palm chats on the island of Hispaniola have no close relatives.

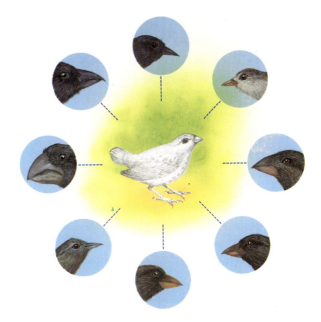

▲ The beaks of some of the types of Galapagos finch. Each beak is shaped to eat certain foods. These types of finch are found only on the Galapagos Islands.

▼ The kiwi is a rare, flightless bird. It lives in the swampy forests and woodlands of New Zealand. Kiwis are active at night when they look for worms and young insects.

Birds in danger

There are almost 80 types of bird which have died out over the last 200 years. This number is larger than any other animal group. Most of these birds lived on islands. Many of them were flightless birds.

Some 350 types of bird are close to dying out today. These are **endangered** birds. Some types have only 20 pairs left. Other types have as many as 1000 pairs.

What kills birds?

Birds become endangered for many reasons. Some are at risk because other animals kill them or take their food. Most birds are endangered because of people.

Many island birds are at risk because people now live on their islands. The dodo was a type of bird which died out when people came to its island habitat. They killed the dodos for food. People brought animals which ate the eggs and the young of the dodo. The birds of New Zealand, such as the kakapo, have also suffered. People have introduced new birds and animals to the islands. These animals have eaten the plants which the island birds used for their food and shelter.

People have changed the face of the Earth. We have cut down the forests and the woods. These areas and the marshlands have been changed into farmland. The habitat for the birds has been destroyed. Some birds are killed by **chemicals** which are used on farm crops. A chemical, called DDT, has killed many birds of prey. DDT weakens the shells of their eggs. This means that the chicks die before they are ready to hatch. Most countries no longer use this chemical.

▼ The flightless kakapo is a type of parrot. This rare bird is found in a few valleys of New Zealand.

Birds in danger

▲ The imperial eagle was once common in Spain. Fewer than 100 survive today.

▼ The dodo became extinct 300 years ago. This happened because people showed no care.

How birds can be saved

The best way to save the birds is to stop the destruction of their habitats. Many more birds will die out if the forests and the marshes continue to be made into farmland. Some countries have set up safe places, or **reserves**, for the birds. Also, some countries have passed laws to protect rare types of bird. These laws stop people from catching the birds or stealing their eggs. Many birds of prey have been saved by these laws.

The rarest birds can be saved by breeding them in zoos. The numbers of Hawaiian goose, the Californian condor and the whooping crane have been increased this way.

We have learned many lessons from the past. Some of the birds, like the dodo, could have been saved. People today are learning to be more careful and to protect birds.

Glossary

adapt: to change in order to suit different surroundings
adaptation: the way in which a plant or animal slowly changes to suit different surroundings
air-sac: an air-filled 'balloon' found inside a bird's body. Birds have many air-sacs. The air-sacs are part of a bird's breathing system
albumen: the colourless fluid which makes up the white of an egg. Albumen becomes white and solid when it is boiled
algae: very simple plants. Algae do not have roots, leaves or flowers. They are usually tiny and can be green, red or brown
amoeba: a tiny, simple animal. An amoeba has no fixed shape and lives in water
amphibian: an animal that spends at least part of its life in water and returns to water to breed. Frogs, toads, newts and salamanders are amphibians
ancestor: a relative that died a long time ago
atoll: a ring-shaped island made of coral
backbone: a line of bones found inside the backs of fish, amphibians, reptiles, birds and mammals
barbel: a thick 'hair' which sticks out from the mouth of some fish. Fish use their barbels to find food in the mud
bark: the outer covering of tree trunks and branches. Some trees have rough, thick bark, others have smooth, thin bark
barrier reef: a long wall of coral which grows in shallow seas near to the land
bill: the beak of a bird
bird of prey: a bird which kills and eats other animals. The birds of prey include the eagles, hawks and buzzards
bone: a hard chalky material inside the body which forms an animal's skeleton
breastbone: a strong, light bone down the middle of the breast to which the ribs and muscles are attached. In flying birds, the breastbone is large and surrounded by muscles which flap the wings
breed: to produce young
brood: all the young birds which are in a nest at one time
camouflage: the colour patterns or body shapes which help to hide an animal's body in its surroundings

canopy: the top layer, or 'roof', of a forest. The canopy is formed by the treetops touching each other
carrion bird: a bird which eats dead animals. Carrion birds do not kill animals for food
cartilage: a rubbery material which forms the skeleton of sharks and rays
cell: a very small part or unit. Most animals and plants are made of millions of cells
chemical: any substance which can change when joined or mixed with another substance
chick: a young bird. Chicks can run around soon after hatching from the egg
cocoon: a case which a young animal forms around itself for protection
cold-blooded: describes animals which cannot make their own heat. Their bodies are hot or cold, depending on the weather. Insects and reptiles are cold-blooded animals
colony: a large number of birds which live together in the same area
cone: the part of a conifer tree where seeds form
conifer: one of a group of trees which have needle-like leaves. Conifers produce woody cones to protect their seeds
coniferous forest: a type of forest made up of trees called conifers. Coniferous trees have tough seeds called cones. They keep their leaves all the year around. Pines, firs and spruces are examples of conifers
continent: a large mass of land, sometimes containing many countries. The Earth is divided into seven continents
coral: a small sea animal which builds a hard tube of chalk around itself
coral reef: a wall of hard 'rock' built up of dead corals in shallow seas
courtship: the types of behaviour which male and female animals carry out before they mate
courtship dance: a series of actions which a bird performs to attract a mate
coyote: a wolf-like animal. Coyotes are found in North America
crag: a high, sharp rock
crop: a 'bag' in the throat of some birds. The crop is used to store food which is passed to the stomach later
crustacean: a type of water animal which has a hard shell
current: the flow of water within a sea, lake or river
debris: the remains of something which has been broken or destroyed
digest: to break down food inside the stomach so it can be used in the body

dinosaur: one of a group of reptiles which died out 65 million years ago

disabled: describes an animal, person or object which is weakened. A fox with a broken leg is disabled

display: an act which a male bird performs to scare away other males. Male birds also display to 'show off' to and attract females

domestic animal: describes an animal which has been tamed. Domestic animals are no longer wild

down: a fine, soft type of feather which grows next to a bird's skin

drag: the force which slows an object down as it flies through the air

eave: the edge of a roof which hangs over the walls of a building

echinoderm: a type of sea animal with a hard, spiny outer 'skin'. Starfish and sea urchins are echinoderms

echo: the sending back of a sound. Echoes are caused by sounds bouncing off a hard object

echolocation: a way of finding objects by sending out sounds, then listening for the sound, or echo. Bats use echolocation to find their prey

electric current: a flow of electricity

electric shock: a sudden shock produced by electrical energy passing through the body

elver: a young eel

endangered: describes any type of animal or plant which is in danger of dying out. Many endangered animals have died out because of people

environment: the surroundings of an animal or plant. The environment affects the way an animal lives

Equator: the imaginary circle which goes around the middle of the Earth. The Equator divides the northern part of the Earth from the southern part

evergreen: describes trees and bushes which are in leaf all year. Evergreen trees do not drop their leaves when the cold weather comes

experiment: a test which is carried out to discover something which is unknown

extinct: describes a type of plant or animal which has died out

family: a group of animals of a similar type

feather: one of the coverings which grow out of the skin of a bird

fertilizer: a substance which is added to the soil to make plants grow well

filter: to separate a solid object from a liquid

fin: a flat piece of skin and bone attached to the side or back of a fish. Fish use fins to steer their bodies through the water

fledgeling: a young bird which is old enough to leave the nest but cannot fly or feed itself yet

food chain: a series of living things which depend on each other for food. A typical food chain starts with a plant which is eaten by a plant eating animal. The plant eating animal is then eaten by a meat eating animal

fossil: the remains of an animal or plant usually found in rocks. A fossil can be the bones of an animal, or the shape left by the animal's body in the rock

fresh water: a type of water found in ponds, rivers and lakes. It does not contain salt

fringe reef: a wall of coral which grows in the shallow water around an island

fry: a young fish

gall: a growth on a plant caused by an insect

gill: a part of a water animal used for breathing under water. Most animals with gills cannot breathe out of water

glide: to move through the air without power. A bird does not flap its wings when it is gliding

graze: to feed on grass

grazer: an animal which feeds on grass

grub: a young insect

habit: the usual way in which an animal behaves

habitat: the place where an animal usually lives

hibernate: to 'sleep' or stay still through the winter. Animals hibernate so that they can survive through the cold weather and when food is scarce

humid: describes moist or damp air. A place is humid when the air contains a lot of moisture

incubation: the act of sitting on eggs in order to keep them warm befor they hatch

inland: the inner part of a country, away from the coast

intruder: an unwanted visitor, often an unfriendly one

invertebrate: a type of animal which has no backbone

jaws: the part of an animal's mouth which holds the teeth

jellyfish: a simple, umbrella-shaped animal with a jelly-like body which floats in the sea. Most jellyfish can sting

keratin: the horny material which birds' feathers are made of

lake: a large area of fresh water, usually fed or emptied by a river

larva: a young stage in the life of certain animals. Larvae look different from the adults

lift: a force which raises an object into the air

lung: a part of an animal, inside the body, used for breathing air. All land animals have lungs

lure: something which one animal uses to attract other animals
mainland: a large area of land. A mainland may have islands off its coasts
mammal: an animal with a warm body which is usually covered in fur. Mammals give birth to live young which feed on the mother's milk
marrow: the soft material which is found inside the bones of many animals
marsh: a piece of land which is usually wet
marsupial: a mammal which has a pouch on the outside of its body. The young develop in the pouch
microscope: an instrument that makes small objects put under it look a lot larger
migrant: an animal which makes a long journey at certain times of the year
migration: the movement of animals from one area to another. Animals migrate long distances to breed, to find food or to escape from cold weather
mollusc: an animal with a soft body which usually lives in a shell. Snails, Limpets and slugs are molluscs
mother of pearl: a hard, silvery material found on the inside of mollusc shells
moult: to lose old feathers, fur or skin. Birds do not moult all of their feathers at one time
muscle: a type of material in the body which can be made to shorten itself to move a part of the body.
native: describes an animal or plant which naturally belongs to a place. Penguins are native birds in the Antarctic
nectar: a sugary liquid that plants produce in their flowers. Many insects visit flowers to feed on nectar
nerve: part of a network in the body which passes messages from one part to another part
nestling: a young bird which is helpless when it hatches from the egg
nocturnal: describes animals which are active at night
ocean: the vast expanse of deep salt water which covers much of the surface of the Earth. There are four oceans, the Pacific Ocean, the Atlantic Ocean, the Indian Ocean and the Arctic Ocean
ocean layer: a part of an ocean which is at a certain level, or depth
order: the scientific name for a group of animals
oxygen: a gas found in the air. Oxygen is very important to all plants and animals. It is used in breathing
pair: a male and a female bird which build a nest together in order to produce young
parr: a baby salmon
particle feeder: an animal which feeds on tiny pieces of food in the water

perching bird: the common name for the largest group of birds. Most perching birds are small. They have feet which are shaped for clinging to twigs, or for perching on branches
pincer: a type of claw used for holding things. Crabs and lobsters have pincers
plain: a large, open area of flat land. Plains are usually covered in grass
plankton: tiny plants and animals which float near the surface of the seas, oceans and inland waters. Plankton is a source of food for many water animals
plumage: all the feathers of a bird
polar region: either of the parts of the world which are found close to the South Pole or the North Pole
pollution: the act of spoiling or poisoning the land or the water
pond: a small natural hollow in the ground filled with fresh water
prairie: a large, open area of grassland
predator: an animal which lives by hunting and eating other animals
preening: the cleaning, oiling and smoothing of feathers
pressure: the action of one thing pressing on or against something else
prey: an animal which is hunted and eaten by other animals for food
primate: a member of a group of mammals which includes apes, monkeys and people
protozoa: a large group of tiny animals. All protozoa are made from a single part, or cell
pterosaur: a type of flying reptile which died out 65 million years ago
radar: a way of finding the position of an object. Radio waves are sent out. When they meet an object, they bounce back to the radar set
reach: a part or stretch of a stream or a river. The low reach, for example, is the part of a river closest to the sea
remote: describes something which is far away
reptile: a member of a group of animals which includes snakes, lizards, crocodiles and turtles. All reptiles have dry, scaly skins and lay eggs with shells. Reptiles cannot make their own body heat
reserve: a special area of land in which wild animals can live in safety
rodent: a member of a group of small animals with long front teeth which are used for gnawing. Mice and squirrels are rodents
salt water: the water found in the seas and oceans. Salt water is made up of many different things. The most common substance is salt
savanna: a hot, dry grassland with few trees

scale: a small, flat, thin 'plate' found on the skin of fish. Scales are made of a hard material
scavenge: to feed on waste food, or on the remains of food left by other animals
scavenger: an animal which feeds on the remains of food left by others. Scavengers also feed on dead bodies
scrape: a simple 'nest' made on the ground. Scrapes use very little nest material
sea: a large area of salt water. The seas are not as deep as the oceans
sea anemone: a type of sea animal which catches its food by using stinging arms. Sea anemones fix themselves to rocks
sea mammal: a mammal which lives in the sea. Sea mammals breathe air, so they must come to the surface to breathe. Sea mammals include whales and dolphins
season: one of four periods of time during the year. The seasons are Spring, Summer, Autumn and Winter. Each season has a certain type of weather
sense: one of the body's natural powers which enable an animal to be aware of its surroundings. The five senses are sight, hearing, touch, smell and taste
sewage: the waste matter which is carried away from buildings in pipes
shell: the hard, outer covering of some animals such as snails or crabs
shoal: a large group of fish swimming together
silt: very fine rock grains which are carried along by a river. When the silt drops to the river bed it forms mud
simple: describes something with few parts
skeleton: the hard part of an animal's body which gives it support and shape. All birds have a bony skeleton inside their bodies
smolt: a young stage in the life of a salmon, when it travels from the river to the sea
soar: to glide and rise into the air without effort. A bird soars by riding on a current of air which is rising
soaring bird: a bird which flies high up into the air without having to flap its wings
species: a group of animals or plants which look alike and can breed with one another
spine: one of the needle-like parts on the outside of some animals
spiral: describes something which curves around and around in circles
sponge: a kind of simple water animal that is soft and yellow. It is full of holes so it can take in water easily. Sponges do not move

stagnant: describes water that is still. Stagnant water is often thick with plants. As the plants rot, they give off an unpleasant smell
streamlined: shaped so as to be able to move through the air as easily as possible
swim-bladder: a part of a fish's body which can be filled with air. The swim-bladder stops a fish from sinking
talon: one of the sharp, hooked claws on the foot of a bird that kills and eats animals and other birds
taste bud: part of the body which is used to taste food
temperate: describes a climate which has mild summers and cool winters. The weather is never very hot, nor very cold
temperate zone: refers to a part of the world which has a temprate climate. There are two temperate zones. They lie between the tropics and the polar regions
tentacle: a long arm, or feeler, of a sea animal. Tentacles are used for feeling, holding, moving or stinging
termite: a type of insect, rather like an ant, which lives in large groups, or colonies. Termites feed on wood and cause a lot of damage to buildings
territory: the area of land lived in and guarded by a bird. Birds guard their territories to make sure that they have enough room to feed and to produce young
thaw: to raise the temperature of something above its freezing point, so it becomes liquid. When ice thaws, it becomes water
thermal: a hot air current which blows upwards
thrust: the force which moves an object forward. A bird's wing produces thrust to move the bird through the air
tick: an animal which is related to spiders. Ticks attach themselves to warm-blooded animals and suck their blood
tidal marsh: a flat, grassy area found near the sea at the mouth of a river. The soil is rich and muddy, and often covered by sea water
tide: the regular rise and fall of the sea up and down the shore. There are two high tides and two low tides, about every 24 hours
treating: a way of breaking down poisons in waste material by adding something, usually chemicals, to it
tropical: describes something to do with, or coming from, the tropics
tropical rain forest: a very hot, damp forest found in the regions close to the Equator

tropics: the very hot, damp regions of the Earth which are found close to the Equator. The Tropic of Cancer marks the most northern line of the tropics, and the Tropic of Capricorn marks the most southern line

tube-feet: tiny 'suckers' used by sea urchins and starfish to move and grip food

tundra: a treeless plain found close to the Arctic regions. The tundra is frozen for most of the year

venom: the poison which is used by some animals like snakes, to kill their prey

vertebrate: an animal with a bony skeleton and a backbone. Fish, amphibians, reptiles, birds and mammals are all vertebrates

volcano: a type of mountain. Volcanoes are formed when very hot, liquid rock is forced up from deep inside the Earth. The liquid rock cools, leaving a mountain of rock

wader: a type of bird with long legs which feeds in shallow water. Most waders have long, thin beaks. Waders include snipe, curlews and sandpipers

warm-blooded: describes an animal which can keep its body at a steady temperature. It does so by making its own heat. A warm-blooded animal can lose heat if it gets too hot

waterproof: anything that is made so that water cannot pass through it

weave: to cross leaves or stalks over and under each other to form a large, single piece of material

webbed feet: describes the type of feet that many water birds have. Webbed feet have a layer of skin between the toes. This helps the animal to paddle through the water

yolk: the yellow, central part of an egg. The yolk contains food for the developing young bird

Index

aardwolf 40
African buffalo 23
albatross 33, 111, 117
algae 14, 93
alligator 17
alpine chough 37
amoeba 9, 54
anaconda 27
angelfish 74, 76
angler fish 76, 84
ant 21, 29
anteater 21
antelope 18, 22, 40
ape 27
Archaeopteryx 99
Arctic fox 32
Arctic loon 118
Arctic tern 43, 112
armadillo 21
asp 35
Atlantic eel 87
Atlantic salmon 86
auk 115

baboon 23
badger 29, 35, 40
bald headed eagle 31
barbel 91
barbet 125
barnacle 13, 59
bass 15, 81
bat 26, 40
bear 35
beaver 30
bee 47
beetle 29, 37
beluga 32
bird
  beak 103, 118, 124
  breastbone 99, 104
  breathing 102
  breeding 106, 112
  camouflage 103, 110, 122
  crop 123
  egg 108, 109
  feather 96, 103, 116, 128
  flight 104
  nest 103, 108, 109, 120, 121
  plumage 100, 120
  senses 102
  skeleton 96, 102
bird of paradise 107, 125
birdwing butterfly 27
bison 18, 29
black bear 29
black rhino 23
black-throated diver 118
blenny 81
blue whale 9
boar 29
boarbird 124
booby 45, 116
boxfish 77
bristle worm 81
broadbill 108, 125
brown bear 30
budgerigar 25
buffalo 18
bullfinch 127
bull frog 17
butterfly 27, 42
butterfly fish 83
buzzard 129

camel 8, 39
capercaillie 128
cardinal 29
caribou 32, 42
catfish 66, 91
cattle egret 23
cavie 20
chaffinch 127
chamois 37
cheetah 23, 40
chickadee 111
chipmunk 35
chough 131
clam 14, 58
cobra 25
coccid 39
cock-of-the-rock 124
cod 67, 81
Coelacanth 75
condor 130
  Californian 111, 137
cormorant 116
cotinga 124, 125
courser 122, 123
coyote 19
crab 12, 13, 16, 17, 55, 59, 60, 62, 63, 65, 75, 81

crabeater seal 33
crane 118
  common 112
  whooping 137
crayfish 63
cricket 21
crocodile 98
crossbill 31, 128
crow 97, 127
crown of thorns 83
curlew 118
cuttlebone 61
cuttlefish 61

deer 11, 29, 40
desert wheatear 123
dik-dik 22
dingo 24
dinosaur 48, 98
dipper 119
dodo 45, 48, 136
dogfish 67
dormouse 35
duck 16, 112, 115, 118
  canvasback 118
  mallard 118
  teal 118
  tufted 118
dune viper 39
dwarf goby 75

eagle 37, 101, 105, 106, 128, 130
  golden 130
  harpy 125
  monkey 125
eagle ray 73
echidna 24
eel 70, 71, 74, 87
eland 22
electric eel 77, 91
electric ray 73
elephant 22, 47
Emperor penguin 33, 115
emu 25, 101, 121

falcon 47, 101, 128, 132, 133
  peregrine 129
fan worm 81
fennec fox 38
fiddler crab 16
finch 123, 127, 135
fish
  bony 70, 74, 75, 90
  breathing 68, 89
  breeding 67, 86, 87, 89

camouflage 76
eggs 67, 70, 71, 86, 90
jawless 70, 71, 90
senses 66
flamingo 101
flounder 81
flycatcher 29, 126, 127
flying fish 74
flying fox 17
fossil 48, 99
fox 29, 40
frigate bird 107, 116
frilled lizard 25
frog 10, 15, 17, 35, 40, 89

Galapagos hawk 49
Galapagos Islands 45, 49
gall wasp 29
gannet 45, 116, 117
gar 91
gazelle 23
giant clam 58
giant tortoise 45
giraffe 23
glass eel 87
gnu 42
goby 81
goldfinch 127
goose 112, 115, 118
  blue 112
  brent 112
  greylag 112
  Hawaiian 137
  snow 112
goshawk 129
grasshopper 25, 37
Great Barrier Reef 83
great white shark 72
grebe 16, 107, 118
ground squirrel 35
grouse 120, 128
  willow 115
guillemot 109, 116, 117
gull 45, 101, 114, 115, 116, 117, 132

hagfish 70
halibut 81
hammerhead shark 72
hatchet fish 84, 91
hawfinch 127
hawk 101, 128
hedgehog 29, 35
Hercules beetle 27
hermit crab 57, 62

heron 16, 118
herring 66, 81
hillstream fish 90
honeycreeper 135
hornbill 108, 125
hummingbird 101, 125, 135
  bee 100
hydra 88
hyena 23, 40

ibis 17
Ichthyornis 99
iguana 45

jackal 40
jack rabbit 38
jaguar 27, 40
jay 127
jellyfish 12, 55, 56, 88
jerboa 38

kakapo 136
kangaroo 24
kangaroo rat 38
killifish 90
kingfisher 17, 101, 119
kiwi 40, 135
knifefish 91
koala 27

lammergeier 130
lamprey 71
lantern fish 84
lark 120
lemming 32
leopard 40
leopard seal 33
limpet 13, 58, 59
lion 23, 42
lizard 25, 39
lobster 62, 63
lugworm 13
lungfish 17, 68
lynx 30
lyrebird 124

magpie 127
manakin 125
maned wolf 21
manta ray 73
martin 132
mayfly 14
mink 30
monarch butterfly 42
monkey 17, 27, 47
moose 30
mosquito 17
mother of pearl 59
motmot 125

143

mountain goat 37
mourning dove 123
mouse 29, 38
mudskipper 17
mulga parrot 25
musk-oxen 32
muskrat 17
mussell 13, 58

narwhal 32
natterjack toad 35
nautilus 59, 60
newt 17, 89
nutcracker 128
nutria 17

oarfish 75
octopus 59, 60
orang-utan 27
oryx 39
osprey 33
ostrich 23, 100, 121
otter 17
ovenbird 108, 120
　red 120
owl 29, 128, 129
　burrowing 120
　eagle 129
　horned 129
　snowy 129
owlet moth 10
oyster 58, 59
oyster catcher 13

paddlefish 91
painted frog 35
palm chat 135
pampas deer 20
pampas fox 21
parr 86
parrot 125
parrot fish 83
peacock 107, 124
peacock worm 81
pearly nautilus 59
penguin 33, 97, 101, 114, 115, 116
perch 91
periwinkle 58
petrel 114, 116
pigeon 47, 132, 133
pika 37
pike 91
pipefish 76
pitta 124
plaice 74, 76, 81
plankton 15, 55, 63, 67, 72, 79, 83, 88
plover 118

Egyptian 123
　golden 112
polar bear 9, 32
pond snail 58
pond turtle 35
poor-will 35
porcelain crab 62
porcupine fish 77
prairie chicken 18, 120
prairie dog 19
pratincole 123
prawn 63
pronghorn 18
protozoa 54, 55, 88
ptarmigan 115
pterosaur 98
pudu 40
puff adder 23
puffer fish 75
puma 37
python 23

racoon 29
ramshorn snail 58
rattlesnake 18
ray 72, 73, 76, 81
razorbill 116
rhea 20, 121
rhino 23
roadrunner 122, 123

sable 30
salmon 14, 43, 86
sand boa 39
sanderling 112
sandgrouse 123
sand martin 112
sandpiper 118
sawfish 73
scallop 13
scorpion fish 76
sea anemone 13, 56, 57, 82, 88
sea fan 80
seahorse 69, 74
seal 32
sea-lily 84
sea slug 83
sea squirt 80
sea urchin 64, 65, 80
shark 69, 72, 90
sheathbill 116
shrew 29
shrimp 12, 55, 57, 59, 62, 63, 73, 81, 86, 88, 89
Siamese fighting fish 90
silkworm 47

skate 81
skua 115
sloth 27
smolt 86
snail 15, 16, 58, 59, 81, 88
snake 17, 23, 39
snipe 13, 118
snow leopard 37
snowy owl 32
sparrow 132, 133
sparrowhawk 129
spider monkey 27
spiny anteater 24
sponge 55, 65, 80, 88
springbok 23,
spruce bark beetle 31
squid 60, 61, 79
squirrel 29
starfish 13, 64, 65, 83, 84
starling 132, 133
stickleback 91
stingray 73
stork 118
sturgeon 91
sunbird 108, 125
sunfish 15
swallow 108, 112, 132, 133
swan 118
　whooper 112
swift 111, 132, 133
　chimney 132
swim-bladder 69

tanager 125
termite 21, 25
tern 45, 112, 115, 116, 117
terrapin 16
thrush 132
tiger 27, 49
tiger shark 72
tiger snake 25
tit 111
toad 17
tortoise 10, 45
toucan 125
treecreeper 127
tree frog 27
tree-lizard 99
tripod fish 9
tropicbird 116
trout 14
trunkfish 77
tuatara 45
tuco-tuco 20
turkey 101
turtle 14, 72, 86

umbrella bird 107

vicuna 37
viperfish 84
vireo 127
　red-eyed 112
viscacha 20
vulture 101, 105, 130

wallcreeper 131
wall lizard 35
walrus 32
warthog 23
water boatman 15
water flea 88
water moccasin 17
weasel 32
weaver bird 108
Weddell seal 33
wedge-tailed eagle 25
whale 9, 32, 86, 92
whelk 58
white rhino 23
wild dog 23
wildebeeste 23
wolf 18, 19, 30
wolverine 30
wombat 24
woodpecker 31, 101, 103, 127
　acorn 127
wood wasp 31
worm 14, 83, 84
wrasse 81
wren 106

zebra 23, 42